# THE PHILOSOPHY OF PROGRESS

# The Philosophy of Progress

*Higher Thinking for Developing*
*Infinite Prosperity*

**Ryuho Okawa**

Lantern Books ● New York

A Division of Booklight Inc.

Lantern Books
A Division of Booklight Inc.

Lantern Books
128 Second Place
Brooklyn, NY 11231
www.lanternbooks.com

Printed in the United States of America
on 100% post-consumer waste paper, chlorine-free

LIBRARY OF CONGRESS CATALOGING-IN-PUBLICATION DATA

ISBN-13: 978-1-59056-057-0
ISBN-10: 1-59056-057-4

# Table of Contents

**Preface** . . . . . . . . . . . . . . . . . . . . . . . . . . . . . . . . . . . .ix

**Part 1: What Is Wealth?** . . . . . . . . . . . . . . . . . . . . . . .1
   1. Looking at the World from God's Perspective . . . .1
   2. Changing Your Attitude to Bring Success . . . . . . .5
   3. Suffering Caused by Desire . . . . . . . . . . . . . . . .11
   4. Accumulating Beneficial Wealth . . . . . . . . . . . .18
   5. Making Progress with Love and Ideals . . . . . . .23
   6. Creating "Utopian Economics" . . . . . . . . . . . . .27

**Part 2: The Path to Progress** . . . . . . . . . . . . . . . . . . .31
   1. The Definition of Progress . . . . . . . . . . . . . . . .31
   2. The Joy of Progress . . . . . . . . . . . . . . . . . . . . .33
   3. The Driving Force of Progress . . . . . . . . . . . . . .37
   4. Realizing Hope . . . . . . . . . . . . . . . . . . . . . . . . .39

**Part 3: A Life Filled with Light** . . . . . . . . . . . . . . . . .41
   1. Living with Optimism . . . . . . . . . . . . . . . . . . . .41
   2. Living Lightheartedly . . . . . . . . . . . . . . . . . . . . .42
   3. Believing Tomorrow Will Be Better . . . . . . . . . .44
   4. Expanding the Circle of Happiness . . . . . . . . . .46
   5. Walking with God . . . . . . . . . . . . . . . . . . . . . . .49

**Part 4: A Mind that Invites Happiness** . . . . . . . . . . . .51

   1. The Laws of the Mind . . . . . . . . . . . . . . . . . . . .51

   2. A Mind that Brings Others Happiness . . . . . . . . .53

   3. In Tune with God's Vibration . . . . . . . . . . . . . . . .55

   4. A Humble, Accepting Mind . . . . . . . . . . . . . . . .57

   5. The Power of Prayer . . . . . . . . . . . . . . . . . . . . . .59

**Part 5: The True Nature of Wealth** . . . . . . . . . . . . . . . .63

   1. Wealth as a Foundation . . . . . . . . . . . . . . . . . . . .63

   2. Wealth and Competition . . . . . . . . . . . . . . . . . . . .65

   3. Good and Evil in Relation to Wealth . . . . . . . . . .66

   4. The Right Way to Use Wealth . . . . . . . . . . . . . . .68

   5. Accumulating Inner Wealth . . . . . . . . . . . . . . . . .70

**Part 6: The Study of Human Nature**
**Leads to Success** . . . . . . . . . . . . . . . . . . . . . . . . . . .73

   1. Gifts and Talents . . . . . . . . . . . . . . . . . . . . . . . . .73

   2. The Quality and Period of Effort . . . . . . . . . . . . .76

   3. Conditions for Receiving Inspiration . . . . . . . . . .78

      i. The basis for inspiration . . . . . . . . . . . . . . . . .78

      ii. A loving heart . . . . . . . . . . . . . . . . . . . . . . . .80

      iii. A positive attitude to life . . . . . . . . . . . . . . .81

   4. The Person Who Is Admired . . . . . . . . . . . . . . . .83

**Part 7: The Goal Is to Soar** . . . . . . . . . . . . . . . . . . . .87

   1. A Steady Eye . . . . . . . . . . . . . . . . . . . . . . . . . . .87

2. Making Progress with a Loving Heart . . . . . . . . .89
3. Confidence and Abilities . . . . . . . . . . . . . . . . . .91
4. The Goal Is to Soar . . . . . . . . . . . . . . . . . . . . . .94

**Part 8: The Philosophy of Progress** . . . . . . . . . . . . .97
1. The Pledge to God . . . . . . . . . . . . . . . . . . . . . .97
2. The Truth from God's Perspective . . . . . . . . . . .100
    i. Male and female souls . . . . . . . . . . . . . . . . .100
    ii. God's ideal . . . . . . . . . . . . . . . . . . . . . . . . . .101
    iii. What is death? . . . . . . . . . . . . . . . . . . . . . .103
3. The True Right to Know . . . . . . . . . . . . . . . . .106
    i. The Truth God created . . . . . . . . . . . . . . . . .106
    ii. Restoring religion . . . . . . . . . . . . . . . . . . . .108
4. Wrongdoing without Knowing . . . . . . . . . . . . .109
5. Toward the State of Arhat . . . . . . . . . . . . . . . .114
6. Aim for the World of Bodhisattva . . . . . . . . . .116

**Postscript**
**About the Author**
**Lantern Books by Ryuho Okawa**
**What Is Happy Science?**
**Contacts**

# *Preface*

To achieve happiness I advocate four major principles, the principles of love, wisdom, self-reflection and progress. In this book, a collection of my lectures, I have focused mainly on the fourth principle, the principle of progress. There are discussions of themes such as wealth, self-development, happiness and success, viewed not only from a worldly perspective but also from a higher perspective of the other world, which may be of interest to many.

This book is a definitive work on the theory of success, which I can offer every reader with absolute confidence. I would like each of you to read this over and over again, and I am sure that you will attain real success and experience a mystical and powerful development of the soul.

Ryuho Okawa
President
Happy Science

*Part One*

# What Is Wealth?

### 1. Looking at the World from God's Perspective

I founded Happy Science in October 1986, and since that time the membership has increased rapidly. In the beginning, no one imagined that it would grow so fast or become so large. However, once an ideal has been clarified and is affirmed in words, what is within will manifest in the outer world, becoming a reality. Alternatively, we could say that what we consider to be impossible is, in fact, the result of obstacles, walls, or weights that we ourselves create in our own minds.

It seems that people living on earth have long forgotten the essence of faith. Faith goes beyond the common sense of this world; it breaks through the wall that separates this world from the other, allowing what happens in the world of God to manifest in this three-dimensional world.

In the Real World, thoughts manifest instantly, and this is also true in the world of matter. Basically, religions exist to teach us the laws of thought. Science, in contrast, explains with logic that a specific cause gives rise to a specific effect, and anyone can reach the same conclusion if they follow a particular process correctly. Religion, however, transcends the chains of cause and effect. The laws of causality can be expressed in curves that are very different from ordinary mathematical vectors. According to the explanation of high spirits who are close to God, sudden changes that transcend the laws of cause and effect are not rare; rather, these curves are part of the true nature of the Real World, and it is the rigid systems of this world that appear uncommon to spiritual eyes.

In ancient times, God created the whole of this universe, the planet Earth, and humankind, through the power of His Will alone. God, who created the entire world by His Will, resides at the center of the universe. We human beings, who are only a small part of this universe, often tend to see things from our own perspective, with ourselves at the center, but this is in fact a serious mistake. A way of thinking based on God's perspective is what we ought to have; this is what we have long forgotten.

What happens if you apply this truth to everyday life? If you are asked whether or not you are happy, can you answer immediately "yes"? Perhaps you would begin to list your worries one by one. But try to examine the causes of those troubles, and you will discover how trifling they are. In the beginning, there was God, and God created the universe by His Will. Human beings are also God's creation and our essential nature is that of children of God. Yet what trivial matters we are troubled by!

What do you worry about? Perhaps it is illness, financial problems, disharmony in relationships, business deadlocks, problems in your marriage, raising your children, and so on. But imagine what God would say if He were to see your list of worries. He would say that time must be hanging heavy on your hands, for you are wasting it worrying about such trifling matters. If it were up to Him, He would certainly solve your problems in an instant. He would probably say, "Do you really need me to solve such small problems? Let me do something bigger. You don't need my help to solve these problems; you have the ability to solve them for yourself. I have endowed you with a mechanism for solving them. Are you still not aware of it? Then lift the cover of your mind and look carefully at what lies within. There you will find a steering wheel. If you turn it to the right, your worries will disappear, and if you turn it to the left, they reappear. It is as simple as that. Do you understand?"

Having gone to see God to get answers, you would certainly be stupefied. Naturally you might be disappointed and say, "I traveled a vast distance beyond the earth to see God and consult with Him, only to hear Him say that I have all the answers in my own mind. If all I need to do is simply lift the cover of my mind and turn a steering wheel to end my worries, my long journey to see God was pointless." However, solving worries is as simple as that, and this is the truth.

Events in this world can unfold in any number of ways, according to your will. For example, after several decades of life, people usually have a fixed image of themselves, but this image is not necessarily accurate. It may simply be an image they have blindly accepted because those who were around them happened to make certain assumptions about them. However, people can suddenly change. Since I established Happy Science, I have witnessed many cases where people have transformed themselves completely. People can change. You, too, can change yourself.

What makes people change? There are, of course, many possible factors, but first and foremost is a person's way of thinking; if your way of thinking changes, then you will change. The type of thoughts you think is very important.

I differ from most men of religion in that if I were to hear someone's financial problems, for example, I would say, "I will not give you the money to help you out because you are the very person who is causing your own poverty." I would say this because I know that as long as a person holds onto poverty in his or her own mind, he or she will never become wealthy. This may sound unbelievable, but it is the truth.

## 2. Changing Your Attitude to Bring Success

To verify what I am saying, I would like to give a larger-scale example. Over a hundred years ago, Karl Marx wrote a book entitled *Das Kapital*, which became the manifesto of the communist party. From that time, communism spread throughout the world until it seemed to cover nearly half the globe. However, since the end of the 1990s, it has become obvious that the influence of communism has been in decline. Communism could be described as a huge experiment that has lasted over a hundred years, and the conclusion drawn by historians is, stated simply, a single law: those who love poverty will be poor.

What is the basis of Marxism? The answer is the justification of poverty. The philosophy of Marxism can be reduced to the following simple, clear statement: "The reason why we are all poor is that someone is depriving us of wealth. We are suffering from impoverishment because there are people who are exploiting us. Those who are poor are always right, and those who are rich are always wrong; this is why we must bring down the rich, even by means of violence and revolution, to establish communes for the poor where we can all live in equality."

Once you adopt this doctrine, you will never be able to escape poverty, because if you become wealthy, you will lose the foundation that justifies your ideals; while you are impoverished, you can assert your righteousness, but on becoming rich, you will be regarded as bourgeois, and as such will become the target of attack. This is why you would never be able to become wealthy; instead, you would forever continue to justify your poverty.

What sort of mental attitudes would form as a result? First you would start searching among external factors for reasons you have been unsuccessful. You would insist, for example, that the government is to blame, that big corporations are evil, that it is the fault of a particular person, the environment, the times, the economy, and so on. At the basis of your thinking is a victim mentality, the claim that you are suffering in your present situation as the result of outside factors.

Although it might be a natural tendency for human beings to adopt this sort of attitude, if the number of people who believed this kind of doctrine were to increase, all positive activity in the world would cease, and jealousy would be justified. This doctrine would lead people to rationalize their feelings of envy and develop ideas about how to bring down those who are successful, accusing them of achieving their goals through wrongdoing. However, it is quite obvious that anyone who thinks in this way could never be successful.

Let us take an example. Suppose a student who received a lower score than one of his peers on an exam says, "My friend got better marks because his parents are rich enough to get him extra tutoring." However, people who are always making excuses, blaming their parents or teachers and looking to external factors for the cause of their lack of ability, actually do not do well in their studies. The students who get ahead at school are those who are diligent, who make a serious effort in the circumstances they have been given, no matter what advantages their peers may have. Children who, on the other hand, forever complain about the unfairness of their circumstances will never excel at their studies. It is clear that they are just making excuses for not making an effort. It is human nature to keep justifying our laziness once we start making excuses for our lack of effort.

The great experiment proving this was put into practice for over a hundred years. Recently it has become clear that countries built on a philosophy that rationalizes envy have all become weak and poor. Some Marxist professors are still denying this truth, but these people are behind the times. The basic truth is this: the world we live in changes according to the attitudes we accept and affirm.

Some people may think of communism as a huge social experiment that had nothing directly to do with them. However, I am sure that you will find many people around you with similar tendencies. Look closely at your siblings, your parents, your relatives, friends, and colleagues. You can always find people who constantly blame others for their failures and who, seeing others' successes, make statements such as "He was promoted because he got in with the boss," or "She is successful because she is cunning." Usually, the people who say these sorts of things have never been successful themselves, and are very keen to list the reasons they cannot or do not want to be like those who are successful. By doing this, they imprint these excuses in their subconscious.

There are so many people who have within a tendency to love unhappiness, with the result that they can never be successful themselves. It may not be an exaggeration to say that more than half the world's people earnestly explain why they are unsuccessful. These people need to turn their thinking around and consider how they can achieve success. They need to know that no matter how convincingly they explain their lack of success, it will not do the world or themselves any good. Instead, if things are not going well, it is important to think about how to improve the situation. Those who know clearly in which direction to proceed for their betterment, who act on this in a concrete way, and who believe in a better future, will find that things improve. It is that simple.

To give another example, there are many people who are unwell. Of the various types of illness, there are, of course, illnesses that are the result of destiny and are unavoidable, but there are also many cases where a person's attitude or way of thinking is actually creating the illness. Those who are sick would probably be upset if they heard someone say their poor health was perhaps due to a love of illness, but it is often true. Many people in this world turn to illness to escape from problems in relationships, failures in business, or nervous breakdowns. They think they will be forgiven if they are sick, and they slowly drive themselves until they become ill, hoping their sins will be wiped away and they will no longer be blamed.

The same thing can also happen at a subconscious level. Some people suddenly start to do something that damages their health, or overwork until finally they break down. As a result, they convince themselves they are unfortunate, that fate is punishing them, and they begin to feed off the sympathy of others. However, they should be aware that in the depths of their heart, they themselves wanted to become ill to escape from reality. There are many cases of this kind.

What should those who are sincerely striving for success do? If they truly want to achieve success, once they detect the first signs of illness, they will realize, "I have gone too far. I need to look after my health, so I must change the way I work by doing this and this." Then they will quickly make changes to their lifestyle, taking advice from family and friends. On the other hand, those who subconsciously love illness are the last to listen to the warnings of others. Even if someone has been warning them for months that they are heading for illness, they never listen and just keep going full speed ahead, saying, "No, I'll be fine," until finally they actually collapse.

This is an example of how an irresponsible attitude can cause illness. Those with a true sense of responsibility will adjust their schedule before it is too late, knowing how much trouble it would create if they were to fall ill. But those who are irresponsible stick to their ways and create trouble for others. It all boils down to whether you have an image of yourself striving for happiness, or an image of yourself clinging to unhappiness and failure.

The past is the past; you may have had many different kinds of experiences, including both success and failure. Even if you have experienced failure many times, there is no need for fear. Instead, be afraid of loving the pattern of failure. There is absolutely no need to use past failure as a cause for failure in the future; just because you have failed in the past does not necessarily mean you will fail in the future. However, if you find in yourself a tendency to love patterns of failure, be very careful. Those who harbor negative images in their minds will, without exception, continue to repeat the same mistakes in the future; they will fail again and again.

So, to return to my earlier subject, there really are people who love poverty. As far as I can see, there are many such people, although they themselves may not be aware of it; you may even be one of them. Many will continue to nurture a love of poverty even after reading this lecture on wealth. They will think, "I cannot be like that. This lecture sounds unrealistic to me," and they will continue to cling to poverty in the way they are used to. No one is to blame except the person who is choosing to live in this way, creating his or her own suffering. If, after knowing this truth, you nevertheless choose to remain in poverty, no one will or can stop you. Please keep the law of self-responsibility firmly in mind, for it is our own responsibility if we suffer in hell after death.

## 3. Suffering Caused by Desire

As I have explained on many occasions, heaven and hell certainly exist in the other world; there is no denying this truth. What is more, in hell, as well as in heaven, there are many different realms.[1] People on earth do not suffer as a result of the same worries; they create many different kinds of pain, and suffer in many different ways. If they return to the other world while still suffering, they go to the kind of hell that corresponds to their unique pain. I would now like to focus on explaining some of the realms of hell that are relevant to this lecture.

The realm of hell that is most relevant to wealth is the Hell of Hungry Spirits. What kind of hell is this? It is a place full of souls who have been reduced to skin and bone, with thin, weak limbs, protruding bellies, and skeletal faces. Of course, their appearance varies widely; some act violently while others run around wildly, their hair disheveled. Some are so stingy they do not even have hair. Some have no teeth, while others have dentures. They are like the skinny starving ghosts sometimes depicted in traditional paintings.

These emaciated beings of hell are all consumed by insatiable desire. What are they most eager for? First,

---

1. The universe is multi-dimensional and the world we inhabit is the third dimension, which consists of three elements—length, breadth, and height. While heaven stretches from the fourth to the ninth dimensions, hell only occupies a tiny section of the fourth dimension. Those in hell have the chance to return to heaven through self-reflection and repentance. Refer to Chapter 1 of *The Laws of the Sun* by Ryuho Okawa (Lantern Books, 2001).

they crave food, but food only represents their endless desire to take from others. In this realm of hell, there is food but it is of a cruel nature, making the inhabitants even hungrier and redoubling their suffering. For example, there are trees heavy with ripe bananas. When the spirits in this hell crawl up craggy slopes with empty stomachs, they find mouth-watering bananas hanging from trees. However, these bananas are only an illusion, yet they seem very real. The spirits are rapturous to come upon the fruit, but the moment they peel a banana and try to eat it, it suddenly vaporizes and burns up. There is drinking water of the same nature. These spirits are so thirsty that they search desperately for water, crawling over desert sands until finally they reach an oasis. However, as soon as they try to gulp down the water, it evaporates and disappears. Some of them repeat this scenario over and over for hundreds of years.

Those of a more violent disposition are not satisfied with just ordinary food. Because they cannot bear the acute hunger, they feel like eating their companions who inhabit the same hell; they actually start to do this and turn into fiends. However, there is no such thing as a physical body in the other world, so as soon as they think they have eaten someone, the person reappears. They think their victim has somehow managed to escape, so they attempt to eat the person again. The moment they think they have eaten their victim up, the person reappears once more and attempts to escape. In this way their hunger is never satisfied, and they repeat the chase continuously.

On reading this description, many may think it has nothing whatsoever to do with them, but those who are greedy and have extremely strong desires to take from others will become like this. To determine whether you are like this, the checkpoints are simple and clear. Do you have a strong desire to deprive others? Do you want to take things that do not belong to you? Will you jump at the chance to take the best for yourself? Is your mind always occupied with unsatisfied desires? There is a high probability that anyone who answers "yes" to the above questions will go to the hell that I have just described. There are actually plenty of people like this.

In the vicinity of the Hell of Hungry Spirits is the Hell of Ashura, or the Hell of Strife, for those who are always accusing and criticizing others. There is one type of criticism that is the exception, and this is constructive criticism administered with the intention of educating another. There is nothing wrong with this kind of criticism; it can be considered an expression of love. However, those who abuse others out of a sense of their own dissatisfaction, or who hurt others to make themselves feel better, or criticize others just for the sake of criticism will not escape the Ashura Realm of hell.

Many of the inhabitants of the Ashura Hell have been soldiers in past wars, and take killing very lightly. As there are currently few wars, the modern incomers fight with words. Some of them learn to use bows and arrows while they are in hell, and try to kill one another. But no matter how many times they try to do this, the victims never die, so they are continuously inflicting pain on one another—until finally they tire of it.

Many of the communists and Marxists I spoke of earlier are inclined to go to this hell, because they have a tendency to forever criticize society, the government, and other people, putting the blame on something or someone other than themselves to justify their own position. I am talking about ordinary people, but there are also those who have a greater negative influence and who go to a deeper hell. Journalists involved in a particularly vulgar, slanderous sort of journalism will generally go to this realm of hell, where they continue to hurt one another in the other world.

Among those given to verbal abuse are some extremely powerful leaders who have been involved in different fields, for instance, critics, thinkers, teachers, and religious leaders. The influence of such people is so vast that they are not allowed to remain in the Ashura Realm but sink to a deeper hell, known as Abysmal Hell. This realm of hell is located in far deeper regions, and is like the lowest basement level of a building. Those who have been leaders fall straightaway to this hell and are left there almost alone, completely segregated from others. The souls who are not so influential are not a major problem; they only hurt each other. However, those with influence are very dangerous because they stir up the ill will of all those around; the weight of their evil is so great that they fall down directly to this deep hell.

Another hell in the neighborhood of the Ashura Realm is called the Hell of Lust. In this modern age, an increasing number of people will go to this realm after they die. As you can probably imagine, it is a hell where those who have made serious mistakes in relationships with the opposite sex gather. Minor mistakes that people make in their youth will, of course, be overlooked; those who have made such mistakes simply look back and repent their foolishness. However, those in whom these tendencies have become deeply ingrained throughout their lives are very likely to go to this hell. This hell is also known as the Hell of the Bloody Pond, and those who are there continue to have sexual intercourse eternally, which appears intolerably ugly to an objective observer; they look like hundreds of earthworms all bunched up together, wriggling in a muddy pond. There are a number of people who believe forever that this is the world of greatest pleasure and thus cannot escape.

A man or woman can easily make a mistake and step off the path, so it is necessary to practice self-reflection. God is not so cruel as to condemn people to hell just because they have made one mistake. Human beings are apt to make mistakes, but every time you realize you have made a mistake, you need to practice deep self-reflection and get back on the right track. I do not mean that everyone struggling in a three-sided, four-sided, five-sided, or even more complex relationship will go to hell for that reason alone. Generally speaking, however, those involved in complex relationships are driven to jealousy, and actually create hell in their own minds. Their minds become occupied with suspicions and jealousies, and not only family relationships but other relationships as well turn into a hell. It is these sorts of mindsets that are actually mistaken.

If there is anyone who can love several partners equally, and assure them all of constant happiness like certain kings of old, I do not deny the possibility that they will return to heaven. However, you need to know that things do not usually go so smoothly because it is quite difficult to control the mind, and people are usually not skilled in this. To a certain extent, it is important to know how to be content; in many cases, the bud of happiness can bloom by finding contentment with what you have already been given.

## 4. Accumulating Beneficial Wealth

Earlier, I described a painful world connected to appetite, but there is also a realm of hell related to wealth. Money is a controversial issue. Essentially, money itself is neutral, it is neither good nor evil. Looking at the economic development of modern society, the effects seem to have been largely good. For example, in developing countries, where people suffer because of poverty, we can find many cases where people would not have created a hell in their minds if only the economy had been flourishing. If crime and disease increase as the result of a weak economy, then an increasing number of people die in pain, resulting in an expansion of the hell realms, so we cannot deny the fact that money has a beneficial function in modern society. It diminishes the hell realms by strengthening the economy, and improving the environment.

In India, Mother Teresa devoted herself to relieving the suffering of the people. In the early stages of civilization, the kind of work she did was the responsibility of religion. In modern society, however, it should be the task of politics. If political systems are functioning well enough, there should be no need for religion to shoulder the burden of social responsibility. In a society where political systems are working efficiently and the economy develops with the support of government, tasks such as building hospitals and providing nursing care will automatically be taken care of. But in some developing countries, religion still assists with the care of the sick because the political systems and economy are not stable. Therefore money can be considered good in that it is able to relieve suffering.

From ancient times, however, money has always been a trap. Jesus said, "It is easier for a camel to go through the eye of a needle than for a rich man to enter the kingdom of God" (Matt. 19:24). This is often misunderstood; it teaches that those who become obsessed with materialistic values, disregarding the existence of the other world and the significance of the spiritual, will fail to go to heaven. It is more difficult for such people to enter heaven than for a camel to pass through the eye of a needle. This is actually a warning about the dangers of attachment.

What are the dangers of attachment? The stronger the desire for material wealth, the more materialistic a person becomes, consequently ceasing to pay attention to matters pertaining to spirituality, forgetting the fact that a guardian spirit is always watching over each one of us with warm eyes.[2] Those obsessed with worldly attach-

---

2. The soul that resides in the human body is only one part of the spiritual whole; in the subconscious level, the soul is connected to its own bigger entity that remains in the Real World. The spiritual body consists of one core spirit and five branch spirits, and

ments stubbornly refuse to accept the existence of a
guardian spirit. If you want to check whether or not you
have strong attachments, imagine that your guardian
spirit is watching over you all day long. Can you bear
those eyes constantly upon you?

Suppose someone was observing your every thought
and action, every day from morning to night—could you
tolerate it? Those who can bear this have pure minds and
hearts. They have no problem being under constant
observation, because as soon as they harbor a negative
thought they become aware of what they are doing and
immediately reflect on themselves. The spirits in heaven
observe with contentment those who instantly repent of
any wrong they have done. Those absorbed in scheming
to reduce others to misfortune will find it unbearable to
know that all their evil thoughts are exposed. Wrongdoing occurs only because people believe that their
thoughts and actions are not apparent, but once they-
know someone is watching, they are no longer able to
think evil thoughts or put them into practice.

If you feel your guardian spirit would say, "You are

---

they are called brother or sister souls. Each of the six comes
down to earth in turn to carry out their spiritual refinement, while
the spirit whose turn is next takes on a monitoring and supervi-
sory role as "guardian spirit" for the spirit actually on earth. Refer
to Chapter 2 of *The Laws of the Sun.*

doing very well. You are making an effort, working hard and saving money," then you have met the expectations of your guardian spirit and you are on the right track. If, on the other hand, you feel ashamed at being exposed, you have a problem. You will know to which category you belong by imagining you are constantly being watched. Apart from those who are barefacedly shameless, if your sensibilities are normal and you have no problem with the idea of being watched, you have nothing to worry about. But if you feel embarrassed at the idea that your thoughts and acts are being observed, you are in the high-risk category.

This is the reason money can be said to be a double-edged sword. To build a fortune through hard work for positive ends can be viewed as good; in fact it should definitely be considered enormously good. Be cautious of views stating that accumulating wealth is evil, because you will be led down a Marxist path. As long as a person wishes to confine him- or herself to poverty that is fine, but if that person begins to influence others, it becomes dangerous. It is important to know that certain kinds of suffering and worry can be relieved by financial aid, as Mother Teresa's work in the slums illustrates. For this reason, accumulating wealth in the correct way, by making an effort and working at something that contributes to society, can be considered right. I can state clearly that this is good; unless you know this truth, you may be led in the wrong direction.

What is more, using wealth for higher ends should be regarded as an even greater good. Private wealth in itself represents the reward for hard work; if you use this accumulated wealth for something more valuable, even more good is produced. This good will bear further "interest." In this way, good attracts good, and happiness invites happiness. This is the mechanism for the expansion of wealth.

Although I do not like the idea of simply dividing people into two groups, good and bad, let us try to imagine there are only two categories. If those classified as "bad" saved a lot of money and became rich, and those in the "good" group were all poor, what kind of world would unfold? Eventually those who were "bad" would gain more power and influence, and try to change the world in whatever ways they wanted, creating a lot of problems. I believe that this world will be a better place when good people, those who have honest and pure hearts, become affluent and influential. When these people gain financial power, they will be able to help guide the souls of many.

In contrast, imagine that the good-hearted live in poverty. Even if they could enjoy personal happiness by maintaining their peace of mind, as long as they were content with their own poverty they would have less means to reach out and help others achieve happiness. To see these people relinquish the chance to bring happiness to others in a positive way while those who were ill-willed and wealthy were freely repeating their wrongdoings would be unbearable. Just as the old proverb says, "Virtue triumphs over vice." Good should prosper, and evil should decline. There is no doubt that this is the way for the world to move closer to God's ideal.

When the good-hearted become wealthy, they need to be careful of the problem of attachment I mentioned earlier. If they become strongly attached to the things of this world, they will have difficulty passing through the gates of heaven. So always try to be free of attachment. As you become wealthy, it is also important to become increasingly humble, devoting your life to enriching the world. If this world is filled with people who wish to improve it, it is sure to become a better world. Even if there is an increasing number of monks and nuns who renounce their worldly possessions, their power will remain limited. The world will experience great changes when more and more people emerge who have a mission, and the ability to expand and use their wealth for the happiness of others.

## 5. Making Progress with Love and Ideals

It is my sincere wish that those who have awakened to the Truth and who study it earnestly will become more and more affluent. This affluence is a great virtue in that it strengthens the power of goodness.

This is the truth from the perspective of the Real World. If you are filled with goodwill and are determined to save many by achieving work that will benefit others and the world, your guardian spirit will become active and shine. Your guardian spirit will be delighted and energetic, encouraging you and saying things such as, "Work harder, I will help you. If you cannot do it alone, I will call for others to assist." Your guardian spirit goes to many places in the other world to gather those who can help you. As a consequence, when you start a new project or business on earth, many will come to assist you, and your project will run smoothly.

If you run a business and are eager to sell good products and provide a good service, many people will benefit. Do not make light of any material object you produce; even if it is just a cup, the sincerity you put into it is sure to have some effect on the users. Somehow things do not go smoothly in a house filled with products created with deceitful thoughts, such as, "The quality of the product doesn't really matter, as long as it sells well," or "We are creating this product at a very low cost compared to the price we are selling it for, but no one knows." In contrast, a house filled with products created by those who are keen to do a good job will be filled with harmonious vibrations.

Along the same lines, it is easy to guess whether or not a small business will be successful. If a shop is owned by a couple, check to see whether they have a happy marriage. Undoubtedly, a path to success will open up for a happy couple who run a business, even if they experience difficulties for a certain period. On the other hand, where there is serious discord between a couple, causing the family constant illness, the business will usually not be successful, no matter how hard the family may try.

The truth is that the more enthusiastically you devote yourself to your work or business, with a positive and generous-hearted attitude, the more help you will receive from various spirits in the other world. The wishes of a pure-hearted person who is determined to work to create a better world are instantly transmitted to the high spirits in heaven. Then many supporters will gather around this sort of person, thinking, "This person is amazing, I want to help," and consequently paths will open up, one after another. It is quite wonderful.

Once you have awakened to the Truth, poverty actually becomes impossible. On the contrary, you will become affluent, your relationships will be enriched, and more people will admire you. It is worth noting that few people who are truly loved remain unsuccessful in this life. Generally speaking, those who cannot get promotions are those who make others feel ill at ease. If you are liked by many, favored by your bosses and respected by subordinates, you will certainly get ahead in the company, and will savor the richness of life. When people like this reach the top, it benefits the whole of society, as well as all those who are working for that company. On the other hand, if the opposite type of person rises to the top, there will be many negative outcomes. Not only do all the employees lose spirit, but business partners also begin to get into difficulties.

Be aware of how important it is to have the right attitude. Even if you think it seems naive to devote yourself to work for others' happiness, I would like everyone to know that this is actually the way to produce great wealth. When you have awakened to the Truth, devote yourself to work for the good of others. Even after achieving success, remain humble and keep on making a greater effort. Then your success will surely continue to multiply until it becomes a great achievement, and you will undoubtedly be blessed with wealth.

To this end, love and ideals are essential. Those who

are filled with love and who have ideals wish to contribute to the happiness of others, so inevitably the scale of their work expands. In contrast, the work of those who think only of the profit of their small company, or of personal satisfaction, cannot find the path to expansion. As long as you aim to make a contribution to others, or to society as a whole, you have no choice but to develop your business on a much larger scale.

## 6. Creating "Utopian Economics"

Now, let us take the United States as an example; as a nation it is losing strength. The possible reasons for this could be summarized in two points. The first is that people are interested in tax evasion. They try hard to avoid paying taxes and the government even encourages this, which is unwise. Tax-reduction services have been flourishing, indicating that people are trying to find legal ways to escape the payment of taxes. Consequently, the revenue from taxation has fallen, which causes the nation such serious problems that it requires the monetary support of other countries.

A second reason for the loss of national strength is that the ideal of equality is being misapplied. Over the past few hundred years, humanity has built a modern democratic society based on the ideals of freedom, equality, and democracy. Equality in this context should refer to the equality of human souls, equality in the eyes of God, or as children of God. When you are born into this world as a baby, you make a fresh and equal start in life, and with no guarantee of any future outcomes. In these early stages, no one knows what a baby will turn out to be, whether it will become a president, a business executive, or whatever. Individual effort, human relationships, luck, and many other factors combine to affect a person's future, but everyone is given an equal start. This is the true meaning of equality.

Equality means having an equal starting point or an equal chance; it does not mean that the outcome will be equal. Interpreting equality as equal outcome creates a lot of trouble. If those who worked hard and those who did not were to receive equal treatment, as communism insists they should, in the end it would be only natural for no one to want to work hard any more. If, after accumulating wealth through hard work, you were criticized for wrongdoing, for instance, accused of cheating to make a profit, you would lose all enthusiasm and stop making an effort.

If the world were governed according to equality of outcome, no matter how diligently you continued making an effort, you would never be rewarded. Perhaps some people would be happy to be lazy; no one would put in any serious effort. It is no wonder that countries go into decline when they allow the number of people relying solely on social security or subsidies to increase. If too many people start insisting on equality of outcome, and taking this for granted, a country is on the road to decline.

People differ in terms of their ethnic origins, gender, abilities, and so on. But in a society that excessively pursues a policy of equality of outcome, the results of one's own efforts are not justly rewarded. Some universities, for example, decide to intake minority students based on a predetermined percentage, rather than their academic ability. However, students should be judged by the effort they have made and not by their racial or ethnic identity. The same is true for the workplace; men and women should not be evaluated by their gender, but by their abilities. Focusing on equality in outcome rather than the effort made will result in future downfall.

First, each individual needs to become wealthy through honest, diligent hard work. Then, using the wealth gained in this way, you must lend a helping hand to others. By allowing what accords with righteousness to thrive on earth, a whole nation will become prosperous. This process is right and we must follow it. Essentially it is not right to run a business without paying taxes. Any company that gathers a nation's human resources, spends money, and nevertheless manages to go into the red should be considered wrong. Any wasteful businesses that purchase unnecessary items in an attempt to escape taxes are definitely wrong because they do not return any benefits to society.

The true value of the entrepreneur is in hard work and making a profit in the proper way, and out of these profits paying taxes correctly, contributing in this way to the development of the nation. Be aware that any company that cannot even afford to pay taxes has no reason to exist. People in society today have almost forgotten the value of abstract concepts such as the nation, society, God, and eternity. However, such concepts are most important. Transforming the society in which we live into a Utopia, an ideal world, is an extremely important mission.

Instead of pursuing just your own small profit, I would like you to be prosperous, in your personal life as well as in your business, wishing to improve and enrich the whole of society. As long as this is your wish, you will never know despair, and the path to development is sure to open up ahead of you. Let us establish "utopian economics" here on earth.

*Part Two*

# The Path to Progress

## 1. The Definition of Progress

The time of progress has a satisfying feel to it; it is as if a bright light is shining through from somewhere and the sunlight feels stronger than usual. It is as if something good is about to happen. Such a feeling must be a sign of progress.

What is the real meaning of "progress"? What does the word "progress" imply? Here I would like to define it.

First I would say the definition of progress is "moving closer to God." Progress does not mean advancing in a direction that satisfies only our own desires in a self-centered struggle. Rather, what we aim for with progress is growth toward God, the Infinite and Eternal. Like conifers growing straight up into the sky, our progress should be headed straight for God. There can be no other direction, and this is deeply connected to the mission bestowed upon us as human beings when we are born into this world.

All human beings have eternal life. No matter how

strongly intellectuals may reject the idea, our souls *are* eternal; we are beings living in an eternal chain that consists of past, present and future. Those who lived in the past eras were none other than ourselves, and we who are alive in the present are the very people who will create history in the future.

The most important fact that we need to keep in mind when we think about progress toward God is that we are never just creatures of chance. It can never be coincidence that a human being comes into existence; our lives are not without purpose. Everything comes under God's grand plan. According to Divine providence we undergo spiritual refinement eternally on this beautiful planet, earth. When we awaken to God's promise, how can we choose any other direction except toward Him?

Looking around, however, we see so many people in the world who are ignorant of this truth and are unaware of the significance of these times. This is truly regrettable. There are many who consider the spiritual messages I publish to be merely fanciful tales or myths. These people believe that their physical existence is all there is; they simply equate the spirit world with childish ghost stories they may have heard now and then. However, my books of Truth reveal that the Real World is, as its name indicates, the true world, and that the world we live in now is only temporary.

To explain this let me use the cinema as a metaphor. A human being with a physical body in the three-dimensional world is the equivalent of an actor who appears on a screen, and the audience sitting back and watching the screen are spiritual beings who inhabit the Real World, which extends from the fourth dimension beyond. We may appear actually to be thinking, laughing, and independently going about our own lives just like the movie stars on the silver screen, but the truth is that the audience who are watching us represent the true state of existence.

In Buddhism, being unable to see the Truth is known as the state of "ignorance"; in Japanese this literally means "without light." Without light, we cannot see anything. What is this light? It is the light of wisdom. Only with the light of wisdom can we see the Truth. This is why the state of being without light is called "ignorance." The grand mission that awaits us is to help awaken our fellow human beings who are still in spiritual darkness. It is our mission to give light to those who do not have it and to share our wisdom with those who have yet to discover it.

## 2. The Joy of Progress

I have talked about growing toward God as the first element of progress. The second element that I would like to discuss is joy. Progress multiplies joy. This amplification of joy represents the true nature of progress. Take a company, for example. It is not merely a growth in profits or an increase in the number of buildings and employees that indicates the development of a company; it is an increase of joy in the employees that is the indicator of progress. The increase of joy of the employees represents true development, while the development expressed in the sales figures serves as a basis for that development. Likewise joy and the growth of it should accompany the development of our organization.

If progress is to increase joy, what is necessary for us to do? The answer is that each and every person needs to play the principal role in his or her own life. It may be fun to watch others sing or dance or play baseball. However, true enjoyment or pleasure is only to be savored through actually singing or dancing or joining in a game oneself. Undoubtedly the greatest pleasure is to be found in actually taking an active role, so if you want to enjoy progress by increasing your joy, you need to take on a challenge in which you yourself play the lead role in increasing your joy. Rather than staying detached from life, I encourage you to see yourself as a part of it.

The development of our organization indicates that each of our members is making progress. The overflowing joy of each individual member will fill our organization with joy. We discourage people from being satisfied to remain inactive or indifferent, like outside observers. I would like those who have come across the Truth and joined Happy Science to awaken and play a central role in the movement to bring happiness to themselves and to all of humanity. I would like you all to fight in the front line, as "fighters" of Light.

Only when you actually put your knowledge of the Truth into practice will true joy well up within you. If you do not put what you have learned into practice, you will never know what joy feels like. If you only hear from others about the joy of knowing and learning the Truth, you cannot progress beyond a certain level of understanding. Only when you have experienced it for yourself can you feel the joy of learning. Only when you try it for yourself can you taste the Truth. The taste of Truth is truly savored through learning and practicing it.

Some people may simply be curious onlookers, just observing those who study and thinking to themselves, "What on earth do they get from learning the Truth?" To those who are doubtful about the Truth I would say, "Please try tasting the Truth by putting it into practice. Then you will understand what I am trying to say. Before you judge my teachings to be right or wrong with the detachment of a critic, please try practicing and tasting them. The answer will be self-evident.

Before you ask why 'love that gives' leads to happiness, just try giving love to others and experience the wonderful feeling that awaits you. If you experience what happens when you do this, you will have no need of any explanations. Rather than discussing the end results of giving love, first translate it into action. It is something you will be able to understand only when you have practiced it."

I write many books on the Truth, and some may doubt that they are truly sacred writings. When conveying the Truth to others, you may encounter many who question its authenticity. To people like this, I would suggest you reply, "First please try practicing what is written, and taste the Truth for yourself, then you will know whether or not it is authentic." If you can experience joy and those around you can also find delight as a result of your actions, there can be no denying that the Truth is authentic, and that what is written has the support of the high spirits in heaven who are close to God. Whether or not my books are nonsensical imaginings fabricated for profit will become clear when you read the content and translate them into action. For this reason I would like you first to experience the teachings and act in accordance with them.

The more you taste the words of high spirits, the more deeply you can savor them, and the further your joy will expand. It is also true that as you continue to refine yourself through the various stages in life, you will comprehend their true messages differently. The higher your awareness, the deeper the meaning you will grasp, and the more you will see the brilliant light in my words. So, let us find progress in the increase of joy, which I believe to be a wonderful goal for us to aspire to.

## 3. The Driving Force of Progress

The third element of progress is hope. Progress should be accompanied by hope for the future. Jesus Christ said, "Make a tree good and its fruit will be good, or make a tree bad and its fruit will be bad, for a tree is recognized by its fruit" (Matt. 12:33). The "tree" represents the present and its "fruit" represent the future. So the present direction, ideas, and actions for progress will determine the fruit of that effort. The fruit will then become the seeds for new trees to follow, so the relationship of the tree and its fruit can be considered a metaphor for the chains of cause and effect that stretch for all eternity.

The development that we have the intention of achieving must always embody a steady hope. What will come to pass after development must also be filled with hope, inspiring people with a hundred times more courage to realize an even better world. Although the movement to convey the Truth rises powerfully, do not base your commitment on ideas of self-sacrifice. Instead, as a result of this movement for development, aim to be like a big, beautiful fruit, generating a lot of joy and achieving further progress. I would like you to radiate a brilliant light, which will also increase the brilliance of others.

Imagine numerous Christmas lights decorating a grand Christmas tree. Imagine lots of these little lights and various other decorations hanging from the ceiling. As more and more of them light up, the scene becomes more beautiful. But as the new lights came on, what if the old ones started to go off? This would surely trigger feelings of loneliness and sadness. This is a long way from true development, so I strongly and sincerely wish that everyone will continue to emit a strong light for a long time, like long-lasting light bulbs.

Always keep engraving hope within you. Embrace hope for this year deep in your heart, and for next year, and the year after that. Embrace hope for ten years' time, or fifty years, or a hundred years after you have left this world. Hold on to hope for a thousand or two thousand years in the future, and nurture hope for those who will be born. The reason I stress the importance of hope is that it is actually a driving force for progress. Hope is a driving force because you have the expectation of joy, that when your hopes have been realized you will emit a more brilliant light.

Anyone who is a child of God essentially wants to make his or her life shine more brilliantly. Increasing the brilliance of your light as you fulfill your true mission as a child of God is nothing less than the realization of hope.

## 4. Realizing Hope

Lastly, I would like to point out what you need to focus on in order to realize your hopes. First of all, it is necessary that your mind be in the right direction. Decide on one focus and try to concentrate your thoughts on this. As long as the direction is toward God, concentrating your thoughts in this way will not be a negative attachment but instead will serve as great strength.

Picture clearly what you have been concentrating on manifesting; look squarely at it, as if it has already materialized right before your eyes. Then say to yourself, "I believe this is happening. I firmly believe this is actually manifesting." Once you have engraved the belief in its manifestation on your mind, do not have any doubts, for the slightest doubt will make it difficult to realize your goal.

Secondly, it is necessary to believe in the blessing or grace that comes from outside of you. The world you live in is not just what you perceive with your eyes; this world is in fact surrounded by the great spiritual world where your guardian and guiding spirits reside, as well as other spirits connected to you from previous lives. There are also high spirits who are close to God. These spirits have a very strong willingness to make this world a better place. Since this is the case, there is no doubt that if these spirits find someone on earth who wishes for self-realization with the aim of creating a better world, they will certainly do whatever they can to help that person.

What this means is that if you have determined to realize your hopes and make every effort to put them into action, you should leave the consequences entirely to heaven. Believe in the power of heavenly spirits. Once your hopes have been realized, give thanks in a selfless way, "Thank you deeply, God. Thank you, my guardian and guiding spirits. I will continue to make further efforts without having too much pride about this success. Please stay with me and guide me." If you are conceited and become too proud of your successes, however, you will find that the realization of your hopes will subside. It is important to turn success into the seeds of future development. This is the attitude that actualizes hope.

I have talked about various aspects of progress. Do not leave your dream as just a dream. This year has been given to you as an opportunity to make your dream come true. I hope that in a year's time you will find yourself shining ever more brilliantly, having made great progress.

*Part Three*

# A Life Filled with Light

### 1. Living with Optimism

Perhaps not many people have experienced for themselves the effectiveness of an optimistic attitude in carving out a path through life. Although people have heard or read about the power of positive thinking, only a few have actually put it to the test.

Having a positive outlook is the simplest and easiest form of spiritual life; even those who shun religious faith can accept this. This perspective is based on the belief that seeing the bright side of any situation and interpreting it in a positive way will open up a wonderful life. Even if you have not been a devout follower of any particular religion, if you have lived your life believing this simple truth, you will be able to say your life has already been eighty percent successful.

It may be difficult to understand the existence of God as an abstract philosophical concept; for some, believing is like trying to swallow a pill that has gotten stuck in their throat. There are, however, other ways to approach

God, the easiest being to assimilate God's attributes. Doing this will have almost the same effect as believing in God, even if you have not studied any abstract religious theories or explored any theological knowledge.

The essence of God is light, in other words, brightness. It is possible to simplify an understanding of the path to happiness and the path to God as living with the dazzling brightness of sunshine, and thinking in a truly positive way. So if your mind is too full of complicated ideas, cut all the chains of the mind in one stroke. Sweep away anything that has become tangled with complicated ideas as if you were sweeping out spiders' webs with a broom.

The starting point is simply to live brightly. The attitude of trying to live cheerfully, to see, act, and think in a positive way, is in itself a path to faith. It is the act of taking God into you.

## 2. Living Lightheartedly

How can we always live in a way that is filled with light? Some people may be wondering how they can make their life brighter in practical terms, and want to know the basic ideas. This is a reasonable request, so here I would like to introduce in a rather simplified form some of the secrets for leading a radiant life.

The first important clue is to live lightheartedly. A

lighthearted life can be likened to the current of a river that flows smoothly, without any obstructions. Imagine a shallow stream, maybe less than a foot deep, in the gentle spring sunlight. The sun is shining on the slow-flowing stream; the bed of the little river sparkles like gold. As the stream flows it makes a joyous sound, reflecting the gentle patterns of sunlight on its surface. This image conveys exactly the light-hearted state.

Picture once again the scene I have just described—the sunlight passing into the stream, lighting up the bed which sparkles with brilliant colors, as if flecked with golden sand. The water is clear, it flows murmuring peacefully, ceaselessly. This is exactly what I mean by living lightheartedly—it is not just a state of mind without worries or attachments; it is also the comfortable feeling you have when you bask in endless sunlight. Rather than the deep waters in an abyss that the sun cannot reach, lightheartedness is a state of mind like the flow of a shallow stream that basks in sunlight.

To live lightheartedly, you need to live transparently, just like the water of the stream. What does it mean to lead a life that is transparent? It means to live simply and unaffectedly, avoiding complicated thinking. Instead of being obsessed by doubts, trapped by a deep inferiority complex or sentimentality, live brightly and naturally, with simplicity. Even if someone has betrayed or deceived you, do not care too much about it; live unaffectedly. This kind of attitude is very important.

Live lightheartedly and cheerfully, like a child who forgets all the worries of the day after a good night's sleep. It requires only a small amount of effort; do not construct complex theories as if piling up bricks in the mind; rather, I am telling you to remove any heavy burdens and make your mind more airy and light. The key is a feeling of lightness, like going out in casual clothes. Once winter is over and you change into spring clothes, you feel light and comfortable in the gentle breeze. This sensation corresponds perfectly to a state of mind that is without worry.

First, remove any armor from your mind and feel the relief or, to put it another way, take off your winter clothes and change into a spring outfit. I would like you to value this kind of lightness of feeling, because people tend to "put on" different kinds of thoughts unconsciously, which results in their getting stiff shoulders from the weight of their garments. Now that it is bright outside, take off your heavy coat and change clothes for the spring weather. This is an image of lightheartedness.

### 3. Believing Tomorrow Will Be Better
I would now like to move on to the second clue that is important to fill your life with light. Believe that tomor-

row you will have a better day; this is the simplest form of faith. Believe that today is better than yesterday, and tomorrow will be better than today. It is important to hold on to the idea that everything will gradually shine more brightly. Instead of worrying that your life might take a turn for the worse, believe that everything will get better; know the day is approaching when everything will flower at once, just as with the coming of spring all the buds burst into blossom.

All the ordeals and hardships that you have gone through in the past happened so that you could welcome the beauty of spring. Just imagine how this will brighten your life, believing that today is better than yesterday, and tomorrow will be even better than today. Imagine this world filled with people who think in this way. What kind of world would it be, if the streets you walked were full of people who believed this? Every face would be wreathed in smiles, and rosy-cheeked reflections of contentment would shine from shop windows. Light would sparkle in people's eyes and joy would well up from the bottom of their hearts. What a precious feeling!

Constantly remind yourself that tomorrow will be better than today. Your mind creates tendencies, so by repeating this to yourself every day, your mind will gradually move in a new direction toward realizing this idea. What is remarkable is that this idea works on others, as well as on yourself. If you meet someone in a bad mood, you could say in a friendly manner, "You seem sad. Why not believe that today is better than yesterday, and tomorrow will be even better than today? Even though it is raining now, the sky will soon clear."

Even if you feel disagreeable right now, your bad mood will soon vanish, and a positivity as bright as the clear blue sky will return. It is important to believe this will happen. Do not let yourself give in to negative thoughts such as "I feel bad because it is raining" or "Because it is snowing, I feel stuck." Instead, believe that the sky will certainly clear and the warm spring sun will definitely shine, melting even the heaviest snowfall.

Someone who is happy can be described as believing in a bright future, knowing that life will be even more wonderful as time goes on. For one who clings to happy memories of childhood but is unhappy as an adult, life is miserable. Similarly, if someone has a successful career only to become depressed after retirement, life is not happy. A brilliant epoch would be created with the very attitude of believing that we are becoming progressively better people and that the world is always improving.

### 4. Expanding the Circle of Happiness
What is the third key to a light-filled life? As I have

already explained in my other books, you need to be convinced that the more friends you have who share your joy, the happier you will be. When two people share joy, it increases, as compared to just one person keeping it to him- or herself. Similarly, three people sharing joy is better than two. Ten people is better than three, and a hundred joyful people is better than ten. Ten thousand people or a million people is even better. When a great number of people create circles of happiness it is magnificent. As the circles grow, happiness increases. I would like you to believe this.

Just as food that has been in the refrigerator for too long goes bad, joy that is kept to yourself will only be lost without anyone else having tasted it. Joy becomes authentic only when it is shared by others. This is the truth. When you have understood the path to happiness that I teach, it is important to be willing to share your happiness with many.

Suppose a tub is filled with hot water. No matter how hot the water may be at the outset, if someone starts to pour cold water into the tub, the temperature will gradually drop. In the same way, even if you are filled with happiness, there is no doubt that if someone throws cold water on you, or in other words is unkind, the temperature of your happiness will gradually fall. What is important is not to focus on trying to reduce the number of unkind people but rather, to try and increase the number of companions you have in happiness.

Aim to create many people who are happy like you. This effort in itself will warm your heart. As the number of people who are happy increases, you will feel more comfortable and become even happier. Do not complain that the world is filled with people who tease you or upset you, who make you suffer or criticize you. You should not even try to shut such people out. Instead, try and create as many people as possible who are as happy as you, and engrave this resolution in the depths of your heart.

Now, I ask you, how much of your happiness have you spread to those around you today? If your answer is that you have kept all your happiness to yourself, that is a little sad. It is like a single flower in a vase, which although beautiful in itself will only wither before long. Your solitary happiness may also be likened to a dried flower or an artificial one, that at first sight appears fresh, but never grows or dies. Instead, picture in your mind numerous flowers growing and blooming. Imagine a field filled with plants and spring flowers, all of them in bloom. This is what is most wonderful.

Happiness can be found in trying to increase the number of companions you have in the light, those who seek the Truth and study. Some people may have negative attitudes, saying they feel lonely because they do not have any friends with whom to discuss the spiritual truths they have learned, or complain that when they talk about spiritual matters they are seen as eccentric. Although some may misunderstand you, there are many others who will understand your way of thinking. So first accept the idea that many people wish to encourage you and share your joy; then you will be able to avoid simply being hurt, and instead become able to share your happiness with others.

Let us expand the circle of happiness, let us increase the scale of happiness. Your smile will make those around you smile too, but do not be satisfied just with the smiles of those around you. It is important to pray strongly that the smile you start will spread to others, then across the whole country.

## 5. Walking with God

Now let me reveal the last key, which is quite an important one, to living a life filled with light. It is to believe that as long as God is on your side, no one can ever make you unhappy. In this world there are a lot of people and conditions that support you, but God is the most powerful of all. If God is on your side backing you up, nothing will be fearful, nothing can ever hurt, sadden, or grieve you. Because God is right beside you, unhappiness is unable ever to visit you. You can only be happy.

Those who have a strong belief in God have Him standing by their side and have the backing of His support. For this reason no event can ever be unhappy. Everything can only get better. This is because these people have actually made the effort to gain the support of God.

What is required to receive God's grace? God does not demand money or sacrifices, nor does He demand that you obey Him like a slave. All that is required is to believe in Him, to be determined that you will live in accordance with His will, and to contribute to creating a beautiful world that accords with His will. No sooner have you begun to pray that you may receive His support than God is walking with you, already at your side. This is the nature of God. God knows all your wishes even before you have expressed them in words.

Since this is the case there can be no stronger supporter than God. If God is on your side and if God is your friend, you will never be defeated, no matter what happens. Believing this is the secret to the ultimate invitation to a life that is truly filled with light.

# Part Four

# A Mind that Invites Happiness

## 1. The Laws of the Mind

One of the objectives of our organization is scientific research into happiness. What exactly does the "scientific research of happiness" mean? It means exploring the attitudes that invite happiness; so in our organization, the mind is considered to be the subject of research, and the basis of this research is that every mind, though separate and independent, is governed by certain universal laws.

How is it possible that the laws governing our minds are common to us all, despite the fact that each and every one of us is unique, and that we have all been raised in different families? If we were to deduce one truth from this, it would be a realization of the existence of the unique being that is God. Because God exists, the minds of all individuals living independently on earth are subject to a particular set of laws.

What are these laws that govern the mind? I have been studying and exploring these laws for many years, laws concerning the state of mind needed to achieve happiness and the kind of thinking that leads to unhappiness. I have reached one conclusion, which is fairly simple and convincing: the human mind is like a magnet that attracts iron sand through its magnetic force. If the magnetic pull of the mind is in harmony with happiness, the mind will attract iron sands of happiness, and the result is many positive events. If, on the other hand, the mind has a negative force, that is to say, if the mind has a tendency to attract misfortune, it will invite iron sands of unhappiness. There are no exceptions to this law.

Let me explain these laws of the mind in more detail. Just as a magnet attracts iron sand, so happiness is drawn to those who wish for the happiness of others. However, happiness will never come to someone who wishes selfishly to be happy at the cost of others' happiness. This law is quite simple, and it is fact.

Some people may think that the world God created is ironic. They may argue, "When we want water from a well, we simply throw in a bucket and pull it up. In the same way, if we want happiness we should be able to get it." I can almost imagine the faces of those who insist, "We can get anything we want, so it is absurd to say that those who try and win happiness for themselves cannot be happy, while those who wish for others' happiness can."

However, I would like you to stop and think about what I have said, and try to understand it fully. In saying that you should aim to bring happiness to others, I do not mean you should wish solely for the happiness of others in a self-sacrificing way and give up on your own happiness. What I really want to say is that the very attitude of wishing to make others happy is the path that will bring you true happiness. Those who struggle to be happy themselves and pursue only their own happiness are actually creating the exact opposite of what they want. This is not the path to true happiness; it is a misunderstanding of the truth.

## 2. A Mind that Brings Others Happiness

The path to true happiness is wishing others happiness. What does this mean? To answer this question, I have to refer to the nature of the universe.

Though invisible to us, a magnificent energy fills this universe. This energy is the power that brings about development, and it never stops bringing people happiness. It is a power filled with creativity and love. Imagine this unseen energy being sent out all over the universe through pipes or blood vessels. These fine blood vessels are also connected to the heart of each and every person, and through them, the energy flows from the heart of the great universe, pouring into each individual. Just as water pipes reach into every home, the energy of the great universe surges into the heart of every one of us.

However, there is a specific method for using this energy. It is just the same as using a tap; when we turn the tap on, water runs from it, and when we turn it off, the water stops. This system may seem unfair, but if a tap is left on, the house will flood. The same is true of the energy of the universe. Though water is by nature useful, it is better that we use only as much as we need when we need it. But one thing is certain: just as water pipes and electrical cables reach into every home, the pipes conveying the energy of the light of God reach every individual without exception. All that is left up to us is to consider how to get this energy to flow.

There are various sorts of taps—the dial type that goes on when you turn it to the left and off when you turn it to the right, the lever type that turns on when you lift it up and off when you push it down. What type of tap is yours? You can check on this yourself. Try simply turning it to the left or to the right, or up and down. The effort to turn on the inner tap must be in one of these directions. In other words, if you maintain a specific state of mind, the energy of love will overflow from the pipes of God's energy, and if you think in the opposite way, it will stop the flow.

What sort of thinking should we use? Earlier, I said that those who have an attitude of trying to bring others happiness can attain happiness. I would like to explain this further. What does it mean to bring happiness to others? It means to turn on all the taps so that you can receive the energy of God sent out by the great universe. This rule applies not only to you but also to those around you; you can show others the way so that they can tap into the energy for themselves. Therefore it is important to teach others the knowledge you have acquired about how to turn on the tap. When you are able to teach this knowledge correctly, it means you have mastered the method of letting the energy flow through the pipes.

What is amazing is that if you try to turn on your own tap for your own sake, the water may run for a certain period of time, but before long it will automatically stop flowing. However, if you teach others how to turn on their tap, a spring of energy will gush forth endlessly, like an inexhaustible well. This is one of the wonders of the universe.

### 3. In Tune with God's Vibration

In the previous section, I explained how to turn on the energy, using the metaphor of the tap. To put it another way, we must make sure the tap is not blocked. The water cannot run when a tap has become blocked, but the water flows without any problem when it is unblocked. This is obvious to anyone.

What causes a tap to clog up? The answer is waste

matter that gradually accumulates inside the pipes. What corresponds to waste in the pipes? The impurities that accumulate in the mind. Though the essential nature of the energy of the universe is clear and pure, magnificent and beautiful, it can be contaminated by impurities when it flows through the human sphere, in the same way that waste gradually accumulates in pipes as water runs through them. For example, people have various desires. Desire is not wrong in itself; behind it is the urge or drive to live. Desire is used to spread the flame of life, and to increase the brilliance of the life given to us by God. Problems arise, however, when desire is used in a direction that harms others.

Although this energy is essentially wonderful, when it flows into the human sphere in its many forms, it often becomes distorted by worldly thinking. Almost all the energy becomes tainted by the impurities of the egotistical desires of human beings on earth. The pipes gradually become clogged and begin to rust. Then the water only trickles out and turns a rusty red, until eventually clean water is no longer available. What I am trying to say here is very simple: your happiness increases according to the degree to which you attune the vibration of your mind to that of God. It is as simple as this. The truth is there is a certain wavelength or energy transmitted by God, and you can become open to this by attuning to it.

What sorts of waves are being transmitted from God's station? Waves of love, wisdom, courage, justice, hope, joy, freedom, equality, fairness, progress, and so on. Only if you really try to attune your mind to them can you receive these infinite waves of light. Acquiring the knack of tuning into God is the equivalent of acquiring inexhaustible wealth.

This great universe overflows with wealth. Wealth does not necessarily mean money; money is merely one expression of wealth in this three-dimensional world. The essence of wealth is the concept of "abundance," and when this abundance manifests on earth, it is sometimes in the form of monetary wealth, and sometimes in other guises. Wealth manifests in various forms; it is one of the attributes of God of this great universe.

## 4. A Humble, Accepting Mind

God is abundant, because He possesses everything. God is the treasure house of all wisdom and all riches. God created the countless stars of this great universe, and gave birth to highly developed beings such as humans, allowing them an abundant life. Although in economic terms the power of human beings and nations on earth is limited, the economic power of God is unlimited. His is the power that creates wealth through energy, wisdom and love.

What I would like to say is this: everything has already been provided for you. You have been given everything. All that you desire is already close to you, before you have even wished for it. All that is preventing its manifestation or realization is your own small mind, your warped and distorted thoughts. This is, in fact, the only reason you are unable to achieve happiness. Before all else, believe my words. As time passes, it will become evident that what I am saying is truth itself.

First, be one of the right-hearted. Detest evil and love justice. Know that love is universal and in this world it is always of greatest value. Affirm that wealth makes this world prosper, and understand that the happiness of all humanity is a prerequisite for increasing your own happiness. It is important to awaken fully to your mission to live for the benefit of others. Instead of encasing yourself in your own small shell, develop the attitude of trying to build a society filled with happiness, hand in hand with others. Utopia will be realized only when people who truly want this gather together.

Everything I have just described will take you back to the starting point. An ideal society begins with an image of it in your own mind. The truth is that when you have established a utopia in miniature within your own mind, then realized it within your own family, it will eventually manifest in the world. What I am trying to say is not so difficult—it is as simple as this: open your heart and receive God's energy. Embrace the ideal of God as it is. Receive the energy of God without blocking it with human perceptions.

You may ask for a method to achieve this. First I would like to tell you that when your mind is humble and accepting, you will naturally receive God's energy. If you naturally love God's attributes, and are receptive and open to them, this will be sufficient to enable you to acquire these attributes. This is the first way to receive God's energy.

### 5. The Power of Prayer

There is a more active method of receiving God's energy. This is through prayer. Some people may not be used to praying, but prayer has enormous power. Prayers are directed to God, to others, and to yourself.

Once the power of prayer is truly being made use of, the world will begin to change. In the Real World, prayers are also used as an extremely powerful method of amplifying energy. On many occasions angels also pray. Through prayer they are able to gather energy, amplify their power, and realize their will. Prayer enables the thoughts of many to focus on one specific goal, and to realize grand achievements that would be impossible for one person alone. This is the true nature of prayer.

Prayer can, in fact, be an instrument for bringing light into this world. So, if you want to receive the energy of God, pray with a pure and innocent heart. Remove any wrong or negative thoughts from your mind, and pray wholeheartedly to God.

Lord,
Please grant me
A drop of wisdom,
From the great ocean of wisdom you possess.

Lord,
Please grant me
A drop of love,
From the great ocean of love you possess.

Lord,
Please grant me
A drop of wealth,
From the great ocean of wealth you possess.

Lord,
Please grant me
A drop of compassion,
From the great ocean of compassion you possess.

It is good to pray like this.

God is infinite; God is the power that makes everything possible. Worries can be dissolved with a single drop of God's power.

Many angels of light are working in this world, as well as in the other, to help realize all the wishes that are made to God. When you pray, angels of light who have been born on this earth in a physical body will come to your aid, and angels in heaven will also start to help you. This is why all the wishes of those who live with the right attitudes and who try to bring happiness to the world will come true. Believing that all your wishes will be realized is the greatest hope.

Now that you have read this message, you are a millionaire in the world of the mind. Infinite riches are at hand. How are you going to use this limitless wealth? You have within you the same attributes as God. How are you going to use them? What are you going to do once all your wishes have come true? When this happens, if you can wish for this world to become even more wonderful, for everything to get even better, then you will be blessed. The seeds of true happiness will be planted continuously in your mind and they will flower forever.

*Part Five*

# The True Nature of Wealth

## 1. Wealth as a Foundation

In this chapter I would like to discuss the true nature of wealth, and this will certainly serve as a clue to understanding the laws of prosperity. In the first place, what is wealth? Is it good or evil by nature? No one seems ever to have answered these simple questions clearly with any authority. Why is this? The reason is that the outcome of attaining and enjoying wealth varies according to the individual. It is difficult to give a general explanation of what wealth and its consequences actually are. It is not as easy to explain as electricity, for instance, where you can clearly say that when electricity is transmitted, a bulb emits light.

One thing, however, is clear. Although there are many different opinions about whether wealth is positive or negative, everyone expresses the desire to be rich, or at least wishes deep in their heart that they were wealthy. We cannot simply dismiss wealth as desire, because wealth is deeply connected to human life itself. All living things innately have the desire to gain strength, to grow, to develop and prosper. There are no exceptions to this.

The true nature of wealth can be illustrated in the growth of plants. The stalks shoot upwards, becoming covered richly in leaves, which then absorb sunlight and store nutrients through the process of photosynthesis. Why do plants store nutrients in their leaves? They do this because they need these to perform their tasks. What are their tasks? One of their tasks is to blossom, and another is to leave behind seeds. Plants serve to provide a beautiful environment for human life, as well as protecting the earth. For these reasons, it can be considered right that plants store nutrients in their leaves. Some types of plants accumulate nutrients and store them in bulbs underground, but no one would regard this as evil.

This accumulation of wealth can be seen in every case. To accomplish work, various elements are required, such as adequate nutrition, strong foundations, physical strength, intellect, and financial power. The true nature of wealth is to be found in the accumulation of these elements. To put it another way, wealth can be defined as the foundation essential for accomplishing greater and even more marvelous work. It is vital that the work we aim to accomplish be in accordance with the will of God.

## 2. Wealth and Competition

In this world, every living being is part of a community, be it plant, animal, or human. Imagine what kind of world would unfold if there were only one human being, one plant, or just one animal. That single being would monopolize all the wealth. In reality, however, a great number of beings are active, and wanting abundance. This is where competition arises. Out of competition, winners and losers are born, though being a winner or a loser is, of course, relative. Winners and losers are created as a result of competition between large numbers of same species who are living and seeking wealth for themselves.

Suppose there are many trees in a certain area. Some grow tall in the sun but others remain small because they are growing in the shade of bigger trees. As a result, there is a difference in the "accumulated wealth" of the trees. In this case, what is just? Which serves justice better, tall trees that grow rapidly or small bushes that stay in the shadows? Which could be considered evil? Some people might start to think about which trees should be cut down and which should remain.

If the trees are to be used for the good of society, tall trees are often considered more useful than small bushes; strong cypresses and cedars can be used to construct houses and to other ends, while small, crooked trees serve only as firewood. Viewed in this way, it may seem that the stronger trees have kept the weaker ones down, yet the existence of the tall trees is of great service to society. That is why we see small bushes being cut down to encourage the further growth of the taller trees. It is done for the greater good. Greater work can be accomplished as a whole if we encourage giant trees to grow and become magnificent, rather than just letting the small trees thrive in great numbers.

### 3. Good and Evil in Relation to Wealth

The nature of wealth in human society is similar to this example of the trees. In a society, should it be considered just for everyone to have an average, middle-class standard of living, or should it be acceptable to have some who are exceptionally affluent? Would it be better for everyone to be equally poor? Since ancient times these sorts of questions have been controversial issues.

In times when poverty was widespread, it was often considered just to resent and attack the handful of feudal lords or local governors who were blamed for depriving citizens of food and money. When poverty was prevalent, the affluent upper classes lived amidst the resentment of the poor. However, things have changed greatly. The aim of modern society is now the equal distribution of wealth, not the equal distribution of poverty.

How is it that societies have become able to distribute wealth fairly? Looking at the development of modern society over the last century, we can see a handful of skilled entrepreneurs who emerged and launched big businesses, enabling many people to become prosperous. In a number of developed countries, including Japan and the United States, a great number of able entrepreneurs have emerged, resulting in the prosperity of society. To use the analogy of the trees, the strong ones have grown so enormous that many have been able to benefit. Under these huge trees, many have been able to rest and receive the blessings. These trees stand for the outstanding entrepreneurs and prominent company directors who have appeared in the past hundred years.

Here I would like to clarify the difference between "money-making," which is apt to be the target of criticism in religious circles, and excellent "management." If the sole aim in making money is to increase personal wealth without contributing to the happiness of others, it will only provoke hatred. However, if talented entrepreneurs and managers appear and establish large companies that employ thousands, tens of thousands, even hundreds of thousands of people, what happens? Imagine if one person were able to secure the happiness of many, and distribute wealth not only throughout his or her own company but also throughout society, boosting the power of the entire nation. That power would not be confined to just one country but would then spread worldwide, resulting in benefits to people in other nations as well. How should we assess such power?

The source of such power is wealth, but this wealth is definitely different from the money-making often shunned and regarded as evil if measured by religious standards. If it is to be judged, such wealth should be classified as good; in fact, by instigating growth it has been transformed into an overwhelming goodness. To put it another way, economic principles that promote excellent management, support a great number of people, and assure the happiness of many have positive effects; it should be considered right to put these principles into practice.

## 4. The Right Way to Use Wealth

To sum up, the law of wealth is similar to "love that gives." In contrast, exploiting others and aiming solely for private wealth at the cost of others is "love that takes." With such a narrow-minded attitude, no one would experience any increase in wealth. Wealth comes to those who strive to accomplish something magnificent with the aim of benefiting others and making them happy. What is more, wealth that has been achieved in this way does not diminish but produces many different benefits, and multiplies twofold, threefold, tenfold or even a hundredfold while the person who created that wealth is still alive. When someone becomes successful, this is a common pattern.

Let me take the national taxation system as an example. A part of the system involves collecting a specific rate of taxation from those who earn more than a certain amount, and using it for the purpose of public investment and welfare. The system of imposing taxes on those who have higher-than-average earnings and distributing these funds to other areas of the economy which have not been so profitable is beneficial. The redistribution of wealth is vital for the modern welfare-oriented society. However, nowadays we often find that the tax system has succumbed to the negative side of bureaucracy, without applying wisdom to further improve the distribution of wealth in society.

With this as a background, what happens if potential entrepreneurs appear? These people could make more efficient use of the wealth that was produced, utilizing their wisdom and ability for the betterment of society. As a result, society would develop further, and it would also become the force that propels business. In Japan, a good example of this sort of entrepreneur is Konosuke Matsushita, the founder of Panasonic. While he accumulated a vast wealth, above all he used it for the good of society. Another remarkable entrepreneur was Andrew Carnegie, who lived in the United States about one hundred years ago and explored ways of using his wealth for the benefit and betterment of all society.

## 5. Accumulating Inner Wealth

In many areas in the world of business, we find those who have been successful shining like stars. However, in the world of the mind we rarely find people who have been successful in accumulating inner wealth and using it on the path to success.

Inner wealth in other words is wisdom. Knowledge becomes wisdom when it has been proved through experience. Those who are rich in the inner world are those who have abundant wisdom. I believe that if the strength of those who are rich in wisdom were collected and put to good use in the creation of a better society, an ideal world would unfold.

Inner wealth is essential if a country is to develop and prosper, and it will be appreciated and welcomed by the whole world. Japan, for example, has recently become rich in economic terms, but in terms of inner wealth, the people and society as a whole are not as rich.

One reason for this is that at present in Japan, there are no clear criteria for distinguishing who is truly wise, or what sort of philosophies are rich in wisdom. As an outcome of democracy, different figures have become active in many fields, including the world of philosophy. People who would never have dreamt of publishing literary works had they lived a hundred years ago can now easily write and publish books. As a result, there are many writers and many different kinds of books being published, giving rise to a great range of information and culture.

In this flood of information, we have lost sight of what is truly valuable and what is not. We tend to judge people on the basis of their popularity, unsure whether these famous figures have any true ability. This is one of the negative effects of TV and popular literary culture. It seems that modern culture seeks momentary pleasures, unable to discern true wisdom.

In these times, I cannot stress enough the importance of each and every person altering his or her attitude to life, to nurture and produce large numbers of great thinkers as in the past. One necessary attitude is a willingness to study more. However, just collecting information at random is useless. No matter how much unimportant information you collect from newspapers, magazines, or TV programs, you will not be able to reach a high intellectual level. In any age, even one flooded with information, it is true that fine thoughts are written and published by very few. To seek out these fine thoughts, it is necessary to look steadfastly for them and to read good literature.

To enrich your inner world, it is also essential to lead an affluent life. This sort of life imparts a sense of abundance both in material and spiritual terms. As long as you are too strongly bound by the material world, your mind does not have enough space. So as a strong foundation for leading a spiritual life, it is necessary to build sufficient material wealth to support your home life. To create spiritual richness, it is also important to stay away from what is harmful to the mind, and take in a sufficient quantity of useful information every day.

In this chapter, I have discussed many factors connected to wealth. Returning to my starting point, if I had to classify the desire for wealth as either good or evil, I would say that it tends to be good. What is more, if it is used in service to the world it will exert even greater power. Humans are living beings and as such, we are certainly governed by the laws of growth, which include the laws of wealth and the laws of prosperity. It is important to live according to these laws, controlling the direction of your life, and contributing to the betterment of the world. It is my sincere expectation that everyone will become more and more affluent, both materially and spiritually, making good use of this wealth for the benefit and happiness of many.

*Part Six*

# The Study of Human Nature
# Leads to Success

## 1. Gifts and Talents

There are many ways of achieving success, and you will find a veritable mountain of "how to" books on the subject of success. I believe, however, that in the final analysis, the laws of success come down to understanding human nature, so in this chapter I would like to discuss how the study of human nature and also human relationships leads to success.

To start with, I must state that there is a limit to the amount of work one person can do. No matter how competent a person may be, regrettably he or she cannot accomplish as much as hundreds or thousands of people can. Of course, if we just look at the quality of work, it is possible for one person to achieve the equivalent of the work of many. In such case, however, the person probably does not accomplish the work alone, but rather is in a position to lead others in accomplishing an important task. In fact, the starting point for achieving success through the study of human nature is aiming to accomplish major projects in association with others.

I must also mention that you cannot achieve success just by being successful in human relationships. It is a big mistake to think that you can achieve success through human relations simply by making the most of other people. Only if a person has the ability to achieve success can ideal relationships be built with another that will support that success. This point has to be clearly understood. If a person begins to rely on others to achieve success without developing his or her own abilities and qualities, that person will experience serious failure in the end. You may automatically think of one or two people of this type whom you have met. You yourself may even fall into this category.

Human beings can be roughly classified into several types. There are two basic categories, those who try to make their way alone, and those who tend to rely on others. There are also variations on these. There are those who try to build a path toward success through their own efforts, gradually gaining confidence through their success and then expressing their abilities further as they receive the support of others, using others' strengths efficiently. Then there are those who receive help from others but become totally dependent, pushing blindly forward and overestimating their own abilities, and this eventually results in failure. There are also some who not only fail but also blame others or their environment, in contrast to those who value their relationships with others and are somehow able to ride the waves of success harmoniously.

But keeping to the point, the basic rule is that it is only when someone has the potential to succeed that he or she will then be capable of achieving even greater success in cooperation with others. If your aim were to find success solely through relying on others, it would be like sailing a boat made of mud; gradually the boat would dissolve and sink into the waves.

To achieve success certain fundamental qualities are required that function as a driving force. In other words, in order to achieve success it is essential to have some sort of springboard off of which to bounce. There are various qualities that correspond to a springboard. If I were to list them starting with the most important, the first element of success would be ideals. Then there would be conviction and courage, followed by ability and experience. Talents and assets also contribute to success.

When you look within, you will realize that you were born into this world with God's blessing. You should always keep this in mind. If you are blessed, God must have given you some of the essential tools with which to live. You need to discover the biggest untapped treasure within you. You may have been given intellect, for example, but there are many different varieties of intellect. Maybe you are good at academic study, maybe you are quick-witted, good at negotiating, or perhaps you have great organizational abilities, and so on. First, it is important to discover your dominant trait, your most powerful weapon that lies hidden within.

What you discover will help you achieve success. To launch a business, capital is necessary. Only when there is enough capital can you buy stock, process the goods, sell the product and finally produce an income. In the same way, having been born into this world, to get ahead in society you need some "capital." This "capital" is nothing less than the gifts that have been left untapped within you.

## 2. The Quality and Period of Effort

When you try to discover your innate talents, you may become discouraged and feel that your abilities are of no value. But you are not alone in this; I was no different. What, then, should we do when we become caught up in this sort of thinking?

When we think our innate talents are inadequate, God will always encourage us to make an effort to make up for lack of ability. On hearing this, you may wonder how much effort is needed to achieve success. The answer is that success can be achieved in proportion to the quality of your effort, and the length of time you persevere. Those who have succeeded through making an effort for a relatively short period are probably highly talented. However, most people need five or ten years, or longer, before they can finally achieve success.

Blessed are those who have an abundance of talent. They should be careful not to become prideful and make a display of their gifts; instead, they need to be grateful to God and continue to make more effort with humility. In doing so, a path to further success will open up before them, the number of supporters will increase, and they will draw less opposition to them.

If, on the other hand, you feel you do not possess sufficient ability, accept your starting point with humility and continue to make an effort steadily and tirelessly. Exercise is a good illustration of this. It is almost impossible to build physical strength in just one day. If you try to build your strength too quickly by over-exercising for a few days, rather than getting stronger through time, your body will ache. If you consistently spend about an hour every day exercising moderately, your body will get stronger without your realizing it. In the same way, by accumulating a little effort each day to improve your work, you will be amazed at the heights you will manage to reach.

### 3. Conditions for Receiving Inspiration
### i. The basis for inspiration

In the process of accumulating effort it is vital not to spoil your opportunities for success. What is essential for achieving success? There are usually two factors, and the first is inspiration.

When you are constantly aiming for success, the very effort of maintaining this attitude will attract flashes of inspiration. Good ideas will suddenly come to you. For example, you will be struck with the idea of someone who would make a good business partner, or see a future trend or a chance in business that no one else seems to be noticing. Inspiration is very important, and if you observe people who are successful, you will find that they are rather different from those who are not successful in this respect. Their circumstances may be similar but those who are successful seem to experience flashes of inspiration more often.

The higher the quality and the greater the frequency of inspiration, the greater your chance of achieving success. Take a company president, for example. An outstanding leader probably has a series of inspirations on a daily basis. What would happen if a manager were satisfied with just one flash of inspiration resulting in just one new successful product? The company would not expand or develop beyond that level. On the other hand, there are people who are never satisfied with just one success that is the result of a flash of inspiration. They say, "This is not enough. There must be more we can do to improve this business. We could offer better quality service, we could develop this company in a more profitable direction." By continuously asking themselves what more they can do, they will achieve even greater success. If you want to achieve success, value flashes of inspiration.

To receive inspiration what kind of attitude do you need? First, as the prerequisite to receiving inspiration, you need to maintain an attitude of making a continuous effort for a specific purpose. Of course, it sometimes happens that a flash of inspiration comes to you even if you do not make any effort, but this is just accidental. If you keep making an effort for a specific purpose, for instance trying to achieve success in a specific field, you will receive inspirations more frequently. What is more, you will be able to receive inspiration not just randomly, but on a steady basis. In fact, whether or not you can receive inspiration depends on your ability to open yourself to it.

The greater your ability to receive inspiration, the more frequently you will receive it and the better the quality of your inspiration will be. Those who lack the basic ability to receive inspiration may act on whims that merely give rise to difficulties when put into practice, and eventually end in failure. Often they discover in the finish that they have taken a detour and in fact wasted their time, money, and energy. On the other hand, the inspiration that comes to those who deepen their thinking and broaden their knowledge every day is inherently reliable. As they put their inspiration into practice and become convinced of its potential, they gradually become more and more likely to succeed. The difference lies in a basic ability to receive inspiration.

### ii. A loving heart

What is the second prerequisite for receiving inspiration? I would say it is a loving heart. If your aim is always to contribute to the happiness of many, to be loving toward more people, to provide comfort and be of service to more people, you will receive inspirations more frequently.

Those who focus solely on themselves will not receive inspirations even about their personal affairs. People live in different environments under different conditions; there is an almost infinite variety of circumstances. If you focus your interest on how to bring happiness to each individual, naturally you will come up with many different ideas one after another, because by observing those around you, you will think about how one person could achieve happiness, and what would bring contentment to another.

In economics, this attitude is called a market orienta-
tion, but I do not intend to provide such a simple definition. I believe that as long as you are interested in others
and your interest is born of a loving heart, you will be
blessed with more and more splendid inspirations,
because your inspirations will be as varied as the people
you are interested in.

### iii. A positive attitude to life

For the third way of receiving sound inspiration, I would
like to suggest always being full of hope. You may have
had the experience of discovering many "seeds" of happiness, one after another, when you were experiencing a
powerful sense of joy, living each day in a truly delight-
ful way, as if staring up at a clear open sky. On the other
hand, when you feel as if you are beneath a sky heavy
with clouds, you may find your thoughts are full of darkness, causing you and others to feel discouraged.

A mind filled with light is essential for getting good
ideas or good inspiration. Just as the sunlight does not
shine through a cloudy sky, so we cannot receive the
light of hope when our minds are covered with clouds. At
the root of sound inspiration is a hope for the future; any
inspiration that comes to those who have no hope will be
gloomy, it will never bring happiness. For this reason, it
is sometimes wise to avoid developing a deep relation-

ship with someone obsessed with pessimistic ideas. No sooner does a cheerful person talk with someone who is pessimistic than the cheerful person becomes drained and depressed, has no more new ideas, and sees everything in the world as gloomy. It is wise to stay away from pessimistic people if possible, or at least avoid spending a long time in their company.

If you maintain a positive, hopeful attitude every single day, you will find that you will gradually meet people who have the same outlook. What is more, people who have a positive attitude will gradually gather around you, because basically everyone wants to be happy. People who want to be happy are looking for those who will bring happiness, so it is only natural that people will be attracted to you if you are the kind of person who shares happiness. In other words, positive, constructive thoughts and a bright attitude will attract others to you. Good ideas and inspiration will only come to you if you have this kind of outlook. This is why more and more people who have positive aspirations will gather around to help you manifest your ideas and inspiration.

What I am saying is one hundred percent true; I myself have experienced it in the past. This kind of mental attitude is essential to launch a business and develop it into a large-scale enterprise. I have described positive attitudes to life that originate in your own mind, and this is actually the very starting point for achieving success through the study of human nature.

## 4. The Person Who Is Admired

Another factor essential for achieving success is an attractiveness of character. In order to succeed, you must be the sort of person others can admire. What kind of person is considered worthy of admiring? Try and define what makes a person admirable. He or she should have characteristics that are attractive to others. What type of person attracts others? What type of person is popular with others? What kind of person can others admire? What kind of person do you hold in high regard?

The first characteristic of people who are admired is that they have ability. To put it more precisely, they have some special talent; they may be highly competent, they may have developed their abilities through hard work, or they may have strong leadership qualities. So before anything else, it is important to develop specific abilities. This means that you must first try to strengthen and improve yourself while developing your relationships with others, rather than simply striving to obtain others' support.

The second characteristic of people who are admired is, as I described earlier, a bright personality. No matter how intelligent a person may be, if he or she is cheerless and gloomy, people will not be attracted to them nor have any expectation of achieving success through working with them. A person's attractiveness reveals itself only when he or she is positive and smiling, overflowing with energy and vigor—so it is important that you, too, are positive, cheerful and smiling.

The value of cheerfulness is so great that it cannot be over-emphasized. Those who aim to achieve success must be cheerful. To have a cheerful disposition, it is essential not to have a worried mind; good health is also a prerequisite for cheerfulness. A cheerful demeanor suggests that you do not have negative feelings toward others. It is very important to increase the number of cheerful people.

What is the third characteristic of an attractive personality? I would say that it is kindness. Even little children are naturally attracted to those who are kind; they know instinctively who is truly kind. Kindness is necessary if you are to launch a business or accomplish a major project with the help of others. The kindness I speak of is not like spoiling someone with candy; it should be compared to a generous, accepting mind that embraces many.

When narrow-minded people are in the position of leading others, it is in a sense a tragedy. No matter how much talent they may be blessed with, no matter how clever they are, or how much experience they may have, if they are narrow-minded and have difficulty accepting others, many tragedies will ensue. This is because such people tend to be hard on others and to point out others' shortcomings, which is like cutting them with a sharp razor or piercing them with a sword of words. It is essential to be generous-minded.

Even though a broad-minded person may make mistakes, he or she will be excused. If, on the other hand, the narrow-minded person makes a mistake, others will nag and blame, not wanting to miss the opportunity to criticize. In fact this is what often brings either success or failure in human relationships, so it is important to develop kindness in the sense of being generous-minded.

Where does this generosity originate? It has two sources—a loving heart, and a heart that can understand others. A loving heart gives to others and is willing to do whatever it can for them. A heart that understands others tries to understand the subtlety of others' feelings, to understand their minds exactly, and to place itself in others' shoes and empathize with them. With a loving heart and a willingness to understand other people, broad-mindedness can be developed to a great extent.

To sum up, achieving success through the study of human nature boils down to developing attitudes that bring success. Once you have this mindset, you then need to value and nurture good relationships with others. This is the royal road to achieving success through the study of human nature.

# Part Seven

# The Goal Is to Soar

### 1. A Steady Eye

When you are experiencing rapid development, what kind of attitude is essential to achieve success, and how can you turn this into even greater achievement? In the midst of rapid development, what you need to watch most carefully is that you are not tossed about by the energy and do not lose sight of the overall situation or the whole picture. Sometimes people get wildly excited, but even at the height of excitement it is necessary to have a steady eye and stay calm so that development will be healthy and continue to grow successfully.

What is a steady eye? How can we describe a steady eye? Of course, the steady eye does not work to throw cold water on the energy of development, nor dampen the enthusiasm for progress. Rather, the steady eye looks ahead into the infinite future. The attitude is one of calmly analyzing the effects of your actions. When you shoot an arrow, for example, you must know which direction it will go, how far it will go, and where it will fall. This is necessary to convert the energy of development into outcomes that are rational and reasonable.

When people get excited, they tend to think they should put all the more energy into random shots, thinking they just need to keep going until they hit something. But it is in the very midst of the battle that calm and steadiness is most needed. It may be true that shooting off countless arrows will enliven and encourage those fighting with you, and it may also relieve anxiety. However, no matter how many arrows you shoot, if they do not hit the target, it is just a waste. It is important to launch an effective attack, focusing on what is actually important, without wasting too many arrows. To this end, the steady eye is essential in every situation.

Throughout the day, carefully consider the purpose of the actions you are about to undertake and the effects they will have. Then, at the end of the day, reflect carefully to see whether you have accomplished your goals, whether the methods you used were right, and whether they produced satisfactory results. If you find that you are not satisfied with the results, analyze with accuracy the ways in which the results were unsatisfactory and think about what you need to do to use tomorrow even more efficiently. This is making use of ingenuity every single day, through self-reflection that leads to progress.

What connects self-reflection with progress is a

steady eye even when you act with enthusiasm; it is calmly watching how your arrows fall, not covering your eyes the moment you shoot. So, the more heated and excited you get, the calmer you need to remain.

To make life shine at its most brilliant and to allow the energy for our activities to flow at its most powerful, we have to maintain a calmness of mind while at the same time keeping our enthusiasm. It is certain that those who lose sight of themselves will not be assured a positive future, and a group that loses the ability to see themselves objectively is unlikely to know steady development. In all actions, it is important to hold to the attitude of thoroughly and calmly analyzing each situation.

## 2. Making Progress with a Loving Heart

The next attitude essential in the midst of rapid development is connected to the origin of progress. At our Institute, I teach the modern Fourfold Path, which is constituted of the principles for achieving happiness.[3] The principles are of love, wisdom, self-reflection and progress, and these elements are not separate from one another but deeply connected. In the element of love, for example, are to be found the origins of progress.

---

3. Refer to Chapter 3 of *The Laws of Happiness* by Ryuho Okawa (Lantern Books, 2004).

Love originates from God, and it flows to all the people of the world. Love that comes from God lights the flame in our mind, radiating out of us to countless others. This is the true picture of progress: love is the origin of progress. This being the case, the progress we are aiming for must always be based on love. Without love, progress equals death. This means that progress is only truly found in love. It is a manifestation of love. In fact, progress is a state in which love increases.

It is only natural that when we want to love others, we will not be content to love just one person, but will move in the direction of loving two or three people, then ten, one hundred, one thousand, even tens of thousands of people. Within the limited span of a lifetime on earth, the number of people we meet is also limited. Living for a limited time in a limited space, every single moment of the day is like a grain of golden sand that is infinitely precious. We must not waste a single golden day. Instead we must fill it with gratitude to God, and understand that love wishes the realization of progress.

Why do we need to progress? Because our hearts have in them the love given by God; we are God's creations. This is the reason love needs to expand and take the form of progress. Do you understand what I am saying? What I want to say is that seeking progress has no meaning if it is not accompanied by love; without love, progress is merely the shadow of its true form. For this reason, at this time when our movement is expanding, putting infinite love into every action we take to convey the Truth is most important.

Put love into the action of giving a book to someone, into the words you are going to say to someone, into a look you give them. Whatever step you take, do it with love. To convey the Truth, put love into the hand you are holding, into the letter paper on which you are writing, into any small thing you are working on. This is the most valuable thing you can do.

Love starts to grow from the small things, from what is close to you. Ask yourself, can you put love into *every* simple action—can you put love into the envelope you are going to mail, into your finger pasting a stamp onto that envelope, into each letter of the name and address you write, into your finger as you dial a telephone number, into your words of greeting? I would like you to be willing to help others without any hesitation, to offer words of kindness and help ease others' pain and suffering. I cannot emphasize enough the importance of always remembering a loving heart in the midst of progress.

### 3. Confidence and Abilities

The third point that is important in the midst of rapid development is to gain confidence and truly develop your abilities. Confidence and ability correlate to each other; where there is confidence you can develop real ability, and where there is real ability, confidence increases. Confidence and ability affect one another, they develop side by side.

What is the source of confidence? I believe it begins with an ideal, the ideal one has as a child of God. Those who think, "I was born into this world to achieve high ideals. These ideals are not merely for the purpose of survival; I am here to manifest God's ideals, to accomplish my mission as a child of God," will inevitably live confidently. For this reason, it is extremely important to be aware of one's mission.

However, if the confidence that comes from the awareness of one's mission is not accompanied by any actual achievement, it may appear to others to be nothing more than over-confidence, or conceit. It often happens that people view someone as arrogant and their behavior as rude, but the person remains unaware of this. To avoid this happening, it is necessary to build real ability, ability that is accompanied by visible achievement. To find out where your true abilities lie, just look carefully at the results you have achieved. Your achievements will speak eloquently of your abilities. A balance of confidence and ability is important as the true driving force for further progress.

To know your true ability, you need to know your

achievements. But what does this mean, knowing your achievements? The best standard for measuring achievement is to know where you stand in the flow of time. Compare yourself at present with yourself six months ago, or yourself one year ago. How does your present self compare to you a month ago? Looking back in this way, if you are convinced that you have been advancing steadily in every respect, including your decisions, what you have achieved and your perceptions of others, it means that you have been accumulating positive results. This shows there is the possibility of creating a better tomorrow, of making the day after even better than tomorrow, and the next month, the next six months or the next year even better.

There is a good possibility that a life that has been building steadily in the past will result in further achievement in the future. It is also important to evaluate your life's growth objectively and accurately. Those who have negative attitudes to life tend to rate themselves too low. They focus only on their failures and faults, where they have gone wrong, as if viewing these shortcomings through a magnifying glass, and pay no attention to the steady progress they have been making. Because they are also children of God who embody a great mission, it is important that they judge themselves fairly, also the footprints they have left behind them.

How can you judge others fairly when you cannot judge yourself? I am convinced that it is necessary to evaluate your own life correctly, because in doing so you will find true self-confidence welling up for the first time. I would like you constantly to remind yourself of these two concepts—confidence and ability.

Always question whether you have sufficient confidence and ability. Question whether you have achieved higher levels of confidence and ability. Although the current levels may not yet be high enough, if you can see that you have moved forward compared to where you were a year or six months ago, it means you are certainly making progress.

## 4. The Goal Is to Soar

I have been describing the attitudes that are important if you are making rapid progress. Lastly, I would like you to engrave this sentence in your mind: "The goal is to soar." The purpose of your efforts has not been just to stay on the ground and run. The reason you have been running and are still running is not merely to run at top speed, like an ostrich weighted down to the earth. Rather, it is to take off and soar high into the sky. It is my wish that everyone will someday fly gracefully high up into the sky, living magnificent and proud, looking down across the mountains, the valleys, the rivers and the plains far below.

If you never experience the soaring, what is the point of success? What is the purpose of hard times, and why are you making so much effort? If not to soar, then what was the point of all your experiences? We have to fly high up into the sky. From now on, make your goal nothing less than soaring. Only when you are flying ever higher can you fulfill your mission as children of God. The core message of this lecture which I wish to convey is this: the goal is to soar to infinite heights, embodying love, wisdom, the attitude of self-reflection, and the will to make boundless progress.

## Part Eight

# The Philosophy of Progress

### 1. The Pledge to God

The title I have chosen for this book, "The Philosophy of Progress," refers to a way of thinking that is quite different from most of the worldly theories of success that are popular these days. To my eye, everything—the earth, the solar system, and in fact the entire universe—is like a tide that comes in and goes out again and again eternally. The life of a human being on earth is very short; it is transient and momentary. However, how many people know or can believe that they have in fact been living through all eternity? When I think of this I feel as powerless as a man throwing pebbles into a vast ocean; nevertheless I must continue to speak the truth.

Many people are too attached to the idea that the earth or this world is their eternal abode. So they can only think of themselves or their lives with a worldly perspective as the foundation. However, if you listen closely to what I have been telling you, you will surely understand that we human beings are essentially spiritual beings, and that our true nature is not that of the physical body but the divine being dwelling within.

The purpose of religion, therefore, is to awaken us to our true nature and help us to rediscover the forgotten Truth. It is to remind us of our real home, the home of the soul. It is only natural that we would want to rediscover our original home and our true selves; for this purpose there is religion and a variety of academic studies, moral codes and teachings. When I look at all the ideologies of today's world, I cannot help but feel that all the efforts made by the guiding sprits of light have come to naught.[4] It seems that human beings have not managed to increase anything except their populations and are now headed toward degeneracy.

In the beginning was God. By the power of His Will, God created the universe, the solar system, and the earth. Wanting a life form that would be able to think and act of its own free will, God created human beings. Our ancestors, the children of God, made a vow that in the world God created they would live with the teachings of God's word as law. On the basis of this pledge, God gave humankind eternal life. If this pledge had

---

4. Throughout history, many guiding spirits of light have been present on earth in both the East and the West to further our spiritual development. Refer to *The Laws of the Sun* and *The Golden Laws* (Lantern Books, 2002) by Ryuho Okawa.

been the kind of pledge that could easily be broken, God would never have promised us eternal life. Knowing that human beings tend to make mistakes, God gave us eternal life and promised to allow us to reincarnate repeatedly on earth so that we could continue to grow spiritually.

However, while God still remembers this promise clearly, people living today, descendants of those first created souls, seem to have completely forgotten it. Even though He could, in principle, withdraw the promise of eternity because we have gone back on our word, God is still keeping His promise. In spite of the fact that human beings are continually betraying Him, God observes us silently throughout eternity, so it is imperative that we remember the original purpose and mission of our existence.

This knowledge should not leave you feeling troubled; I am simply saying that we are not beings created by chance, accidentally broken into fragments like pieces of pottery. The point is that once we become aware of the fact that our true nature is that of the soul, which is eternal, the value we place on life changes completely. When you realize this truth, the value of your life is transformed as if from an imitation gem to a genuine diamond. In actual fact, your existence is essentially a diamond but you yourself have mistakenly viewed it as something of lesser value. Once you become aware of this wrong view, the light of truth will shine.

I must repeat over and over that although this world may seem to be your eternal home, it is a place you will eventually leave. Not one of you reading this book will still be alive a hundred years from now. This is not the world you truly belong to; your original home is of the home of the soul, which you journeyed from decades ago to be born into this world.

## 2. The Truth from God's Perspective
### i. Male and female souls

Today in the field of medicine there are so many brilliant researchers, people who study day and night. But how sad that many of these academics, no matter how hard they study, cannot understand the simple truth that a human being exists as a soul before it is born from its mother's womb. Why can they not understand that the soul continues to exist after death, and that there is another world to which it returns?

The soul of a baby exists even before the fetus starts growing in the mother's womb, and before being born into this world all souls make a life plan. In fact the male soul and the female soul are spiritually different, independent of physical gender differences. Many advanced souls have clearly developed male or female spiritual qualities.

A human soul is not a single entity but part of a group of six spirits. This group consists of one core spirit, which possesses the highest level of spiritual awareness, and five branch spirits. These six souls take turns reincarnating into this world once every few hundred years, and all six souls share the harvest of experience that each gathers on earth; this is accumulated as wisdom for the soul group.

More highly developed souls usually form groups that consist entirely of male souls or female souls; they undergo spiritual refinement continuously, having a specific mission to fulfill in the best possible way as either male or female. However, there are also souls who form groups consisting of both male and female souls. Many of these souls are to be found in the Astral Realm of the fourth dimension and the Realm of the Good in the fifth dimension. Not recognizing the distinctions that exist between male and female spiritual qualities, they reincarnate into this world as alternately male or female.

Some people are born into a physical body unaware of spiritual truth, and deny their feminine or masculine qualities, or strive to imitate the traits of the opposite sex in a superficial way. They may have forgotten the essential mission of their soul.

## ii. God's ideal

Although democracy is seen as embodying the highest

values of contemporary society, viewed through God's eyes certain aspects need questioning. Principally because of the vow we have made to abide by God's laws, human beings are allowed to undertake eternal spiritual refinement through reincarnating countless times. However, having forgotten this, we have lost our standards for measuring what is right and wrong, instead relying on the consensus of the majority to determine this.

If this trend continues, the world will gradually be overwhelmed by negative thoughts attuned to hell, because there are currently more people on earth from the lower spiritual realms than from the higher ones. This accords with the current perception that we are actually on the verge of collapse, although on the surface we appear to be flourishing.

Before we adopt democracy, we must clearly acknowledge the existence of God, because only with the foundation of a pledge to pursue what is right and to strive to improve ourselves, with God as our ideal, can the opinions of the majority move closer to what is right. Only when everyone is living their lives following God's teachings and aspiring to realize God's ideals in this world will the thoughts of the majority come closer to the ideal. In this way a wonderful world will be created.

However, if this foundation is lost, what will happen? If all decisions were made according to the egotism of the ruling majority, this would be dangerous. We are now standing at the crossroads of an era.

### iii. What is death?

Returning to the subject of modern medicine, still many people remain unaware that there is life after death. This is plain ignorance, for it was accepted as fact two thousand, even ten thousand years ago. People in these times who on the surface appear to be highly intelligent simply do not know this. It really makes us doubt the criteria for intelligence. We must be aware that something is seriously wrong.

The same is true of the issue of brain death, often a subject for debate these days. People seem to have lost sight of the true meaning of life. They mistakenly believe that life is only a cerebral functioning, the working of internal organs, and the circulation of blood. However, the truth is that we have a soul and the soul is in fact our true nature. Therefore life must be viewed from the perspective of the soul.

Those who are dying need to make preparations to depart for the other world. But do we see the dead as no more than mounds of earth? If so, this is regrettable. Death does not occur when our brain waves cease, or when the heart stops beating. The true moment of death is when the soul that dwells within the physical body leaves the body, and the silver cord connecting the two is cut.[5] Once the silver cord has been cut, the soul cannot return to the body.

Many near-death experiences are being reported these days. For example, people undergoing surgery in hospitals sometimes witness the operation being performed on them. Some see heavenly landscapes but then miraculously return to this world to continue living. Some people believe this kind of near-death experience is real while others regard it as simply illusion. Nonetheless, I must make it clear that these near-death experiences, which are occurring in every part of the world, are actually planned by high spirits in the other world. They help these events happen to teach us that souls and the other world really do exist.

Generally, when a person is dying of an illness, the soul is also suffering in the same way. If the body suffers from heart disease, the soul will also have heart trouble. When a person's body is ravaged by cancer, the person's soul also feels this pain. In this way, the truth is that the body and soul go through the same experience while we undergo spiritual refinement on earth. So the reason we feel no pain during near-death experiences is a result of

---

5. Refer to Chapter 1 of *The Golden Laws*.

the help of angels of light from the other world; usually the soul is not able to leave the physical body easily.

At the time of death, a person's soul feels the same pain as the physical body, and then it gradually becomes aware of its own independent existence. At this time, souls that are destined to go to hell have great difficulty leaving their bodies. These souls belong to people who believe that after death there is nothing, so they have a strong attachment to their body. They may not understand that they have died until their body is cremated, and even after that some still do not understand.

On the other hand, those who go straight back to the other world after death are those who have studied and understood the Truth, who were in constant contact with their guardian and guiding spirits while they were alive. These guardian and guiding spirits will come and help a soul to leave the body smoothly. However, a large number of people do not understand this truth because they do not believe in the other world, or in the existence of either the soul or the divine. Unaware of the meaning of death, they have no alternative but to cling to the physical body, and continue wandering the earth, not knowing where to go.

As for the argument about organ transplants after brain death, if someone donates an organ to extend another's life with an understanding of the Truth, this can be considered honorable, the act of an angel. However, if the donor does not believe in life after death, both the doctor and patient are making a crucial mistake. The doctor's actions could constitute murder, or, if carried out with the patient's agreement, assisted suicide. Ignorant of the truth, doctors transplant organs in the name of medical progress, preventing large numbers of people from returning smoothly to the other world. This is a very regrettable situation. It is quite surprising that intellectuals today do not seem to understand this fact, which from the point of view of those who know the Truth is common sense.

### 3. The True Right to Know
### i. The Truth God created

The problem with regard to democracy is similar. What constitutes democracy is the right of each member of society to participate in the decision-making process. In order to ensure the awareness of the people, their right to know what is happening must be assured. Without this assurance, people cannot make decisions, and this has put those who protect the right to know in a secure position. This is how the media has become so influential and the reason journalism earns respect. But now those with the information proclaim themselves to be the guardians of democracy.

However, there is another trap here. Actions that

ignore the original promise human beings have made to God will provoke an immense reaction. The Truth that God created cannot be altered by His children, human beings, because Truth is the fundamental law of the universe, which has been in existence from the beginning of time. Just as mathematics cannot exist without theorems or axioms, so sound human activity and social development cannot exist if fundamental and universal laws of Truth are not observed. Instead of progress there can only be destruction, and what people believe to be social evolution or progress may actually be a path to confusion.

As a result, very few people working in the field of journalism today return to heaven after they die; more and more go to hell realms because the world in which they are living is already turning into a hellish Ashura Realm, the Realm of Strife.

What kind of world is the Ashura Realm? It is a world of fighting and destruction. While the efforts of journalists to expose injustice are acceptable, entrapping and judging people merely for the sake of sensation, regardless of right and wrong, is not. Under the pretext of investigating injustice, journalists act in ways that would hurt others, while claiming that the raising of issues is the essence of journalism. In fact, these journalists are on a slippery slope to hell.

How can people like this build the foundations of

democracy? How can the majority be expected to form sound opinions? This is a serious problem. It cannot be helped if these journalists go to hell, but they have no right to pull innocent people down with them.

God's Law cannot be changed by human beings, it can only be changed by God, the creator of the Law. Unless God changes the Law, we humans have to live in the best way we are able in accordance with it.

Satan is the one who thinks he can alter God's Law for his own convenience, for this is the way that devils think. They do not abide by God's rules. Satan and his devils live however they choose, behaving in whatever way they wish and insisting that it is God who is wrong. This is the true nature of devils dwelling in hell. They are wrong in that they have forgotten the promise they made at the beginning. They have lost sight of the Truth and become arrogant; that is their sin.

## ii. Restoring religion

It is natural that we have a desire to know about the world we are originally from. The true right to know is the right to know about the other world and the essential nature of human beings. Unless we know what happens when we die and what sort of life awaits us, it is difficult to live in the best way possible on earth. This concern about death is natural.

However, there is nothing to answer this basic need of ordinary people. Neither education nor morals provide answers. Nowadays, little importance is placed on religion, and it is not taken seriously.

The purpose of religion is to teach what is most valuable and most important, but people today seem to have forgotten this. We are living in a world where values have been reversed. It is filled with confusion and negative thoughts, and we are gradually being poisoned by this harmful thinking in our everyday lives. Some may believe they are unaffected, but just as fish are poisoned by a polluted river into which industrial waste flows, little by little we cannot avoid being contaminated.

That is why the restoration of religion is vital now. It is especially important that teachings of the Truth be revealed, and that people study them. The work of conveying the Truth to the world is far more important than all the work done by all the companies throughout the world.

### 4. Wrongdoing without Knowing

Although I do not know the exact numbers of people who die each year, supposing it is one million, more than half will go to the realm known as hell. That is over five hundred thousand people. Some have already gone and others are on their way. Every year, while you are enjoying a relaxed life, focused on yourself, hundreds of thousands of people are headed for hell.

Of those who go to hell, very few were aware of the Truth when they were alive. It is rather difficult to choose the wrong path in life if you have a knowledge of the Truth. These people lived their lives wrongly out of ignorance. The weight of sin that is committed unconsciously is enormous.

People tend to think of hell as a kind of myth created by religion, to educate through threats and fear. But hell actually exists. All of the hells referred to in Buddhism actually exist in the way that they are described.

I see people suffering in hell every day. It is pitiful; they hardly look human. Once they wore business suits and ties, had social status and earned large incomes during their lives on earth. However, after they left their physical bodies to return to the other world, their mind itself will be their sole existence, so these people who had always harbored negative thoughts took on a form that was an exact manifestation of the characteristics of their own mind.

No matter how beautiful a woman may appear to be in this world, if her mind is filled with malicious thoughts and she lives in a wrong way, her mind will be exposed as it actually is once death separates the body from the soul. The beautiful form will immediately become ugly. On the other hand, if a woman is not so beautiful in this world, but lives rightly, with a strong faith and abundant love for others, after death she will be transformed into a beautiful form that emanates a divine light, corresponding to the state of her mind. The same applies to men as well. So to see the beauty of others, you should look into the heart, for that is what determines a person's future appearance.

Likewise, those who are clever and talented, who lead others with love and contribute to the betterment of society, will return to what we call the Light Realm in the six-dimensional world after death. This is a world where people who can guide others live, those who have something to teach others, and who have a mind that is pure and righteous. However, there are certain political leaders, teachers, and business executives who live wrongly in their minds; they become obsessed with egotistical thoughts and greedy for power. They drag others down relentlessly, criticizing bitterly and leading many astray. No matter how clever and talented these people may be, they cannot escape the depths of the hell known as Abysmal Hell. After death, people go to a place that corresponds to their own state of mind.

To paint a more graphic picture of this Abysmal Hell, some spirits sink deep into marshes in a world that is pitch-black, while others become trapped and immobile in caves. Some wander endlessly in a dark desert, never encountering another soul. This is a hell of solitude. There is also a very harsh region known as the Hell of Agonizing Cries. Those who have fallen to this hell are continuously tortured and punished without reprieve. In a sense, this torture is self-created through self-punishment and self-accusation; it is caused by a person's thoughts, which have degraded and misguided a great number of others during that person's life.

There is also a hell where those living today often go, called the Hell of Beasts, or the hell of animals. The spirits who live there take on animal form. I have seen an old woman, who was once human, writhing in the form of a big snake. Sometimes she comes out into this world and torments the living, coiling herself around their necks and waists. Her spiritual body no longer takes the form of a human being, but of an animal.

Many animal spirits, such as snakes and foxes, have been witnessed in connection with different spiritual phenomena. However, the essential nature of these spirits is not animal, but that of a human spirit that has regressed. Because the human mind has metamorphosed into the mind of a beast, the spirit also changes into the shape that depicts that state of mind. This is the realm of hell where many people go today, as they have lost a state of mind that is truly human, and instead live in an animalistic way. Living solely to satisfy their greed without any self-control is no different from the behavior of an animal; these people have to face themselves in animal form, and reflect on their thoughts and deeds.

I really want to prevent people from falling to such places. If more than half of the deceased go to such places, it is only natural that we, as fellow humans, should warn them of the danger. There is nothing worse than shutting one's eyes to people who are about to cross a busy road on a red signal, or about to fall over a cliff. We cannot possibly ignore them and not offer a helping hand.

A significant number of people will suffer in hell for decades, or hundreds of years after their death. By telling them the Truth while they are alive and guiding them to lead a life based on the Truth, we can relieve their agony. Isn't this the meaning of human dignity?

Hell is not a punishment or torture; it is something created by our own minds. In this material world, our thoughts do not manifest easily; in the other world, however, they manifest instantly. As fellow human beings living in the same era, it is natural to want to save others from future suffering. Whether or not you choose to be skeptical is up to you, but the truth is the truth. The other world exists and I am in contact with that world every single day. There is no room for doubt; what I am telling you is one hundred percent true.

If contemporary atheists go to hell without any knowledge of the existence of the soul or the other world, how can they be saved? The only way to salvation is to enter the right path. There is no other way except correcting your mind and striving to develop in the direction of God. If you do not know God's laws, there is nothing you can do; it is like being lost in a maze. That is why it is essential to learn the Truth while you are still alive.

## 5. Toward the State of Arhat

Now, let us turn our eyes to the heavenly world. There is a beautiful place where plants and flowers of different kinds bloom in great profusion. This is called the Astral Realm, and it is located in the fourth-dimensional Posthumous Realm, a world that is much more beautiful than this one.

The fifth-dimensional world is called the Realm of the Good, where good-natured people go. Those who have lived their married lives in harmony and worked earnestly at their vocation will return to this world. Most earthly jobs are represented there; souls are still engaged in agriculture, commerce and a variety of other occupations, and a large number of couples are living happily in that realm. Those who have led honest, sound lives without reproach and whose relationships have been harmonious will most likely return there. The fifth-dimensional world is far more peaceful and beautiful than this world; there everyone is kind, no one harms anyone.

Above this is the Light Realm of the sixth dimension. As I have mentioned before, this is where people who teach others often go. This does not only mean school-teachers, but also includes those who are able to guide others, telling them of philosophies of life and indicating the right path.

Within this sixth-dimensional realm there are many different levels; it is full of people of outstanding character and ability. You may have had the experience of meeting a group of eminent people, feeling stimulated to learn more and become like them. Encounters with such people await you in the sixth-dimensional world. There, you have numerous opportunities to learn from others. The brilliance of the light there is stronger and more beautiful than in the fifth-dimensional world.

In the upper part of this sixth-dimensional world is the realm of Arhat.[6] This realm is for souls who have the potential to become angels of light, who have removed the clouds covering their minds, lived with the right mind, and devoted themselves to the pursuit of the true path. The way of Arhat is open to everyone equally in

6. The Japanese word for Arhat is Arakan. For more information about Arhat, please refer to Chapter 6 of *The Essence of Buddha* by Ryuho Okawa (Time Warner Books, 2002).

this life. Everyone can reach this level if they awaken to the Truth, believe in God and strive for spiritual refinement during their lifetime.

## 6. Aim for the World of Bodhisattva

The next world is the seventh-dimensional world called the Realm of Bodhisattva (angel of light).[7] Above this lies the eighth-dimensional Tathagata Realm,[8] and then the ninth-dimensional Cosmic Realm or the Sun Realm, where the Great Tathagata live. This is the world of the Savior. Most people cannot go beyond the eighth-dimensional world, since to enter it requires a considerable amount of spiritual discipline. What I would like to encourage you to do is to aim to return to the seventh-dimensional Bodhisattva Realm.

I guarantee that the world after death does exist; we definitely return to a specific place. The world you are going to must not be a hell—a desert or a marsh, or the world of beasts, where people kill one another in battle or constantly treat one another harshly. At the very least, you must return to the sixth-dimensional Light Realm where those who are worthy of admiration reside, and if possible, aim to return to the Bodhisattva Realm of the seventh dimension.

---

7. The Japanese word for Bodhisattva is Bosatsu.
8. The Japanese word for Tathagata is Nyorai.

That realm is a truly beautiful world, filled with a brilliant light. To the eyes of people on earth, roads in the seventh dimension look as if they are paved with diamonds, and the houses made of jewels. The Bodhisattva Realm is a very international community where souls of various nationalities live as friends, irrespective of religious belief. The only difference is in their spiritual teachers; some are studying Christianity, with Jesus as their guide, while others are following Buddhism with Shakyamuni Buddha.

However, they would never hurt, shun or insult another on account of these differences. Even though their guides may be different, they share the same understanding. Each has his or her own role, and they are all good companions. On earth they may have not understood one another because of their different religious beliefs, but upon returning to the Real World, they live in harmony, understanding their different roles.

Those in the Bodhisattva Realm spend their days gloriously in a very beautiful world. In most cases their daily routine begins with a morning prayer to Divinity. Every morning they pray, "God, thank you for giving us a mission that is so valuable. Please help us do good work and guide many." Then they begin their work.

Among them are some who come to earth to guide others, which is an arduous task, full of difficulties and often almost fruitless from the perspective of the other world. Others conduct research into philosophies and technologies that will help to develop the earth. Some Bodhisattva visit hell, and their vocation is to lead lost spirits out of there. Some have the role of persuading and guiding the spirits that have just arrived in the other world after departing this one. Others visit the lower heavenly realms to teach spirits, as in school. All the work of Bodhisattva revolves around teaching and guiding others.

At times, they assemble to study together. Occasionally, teachers come from the Tathagata Realm to give lectures. All Bodhisattva are filled with gratitude to God, and work extremely hard every day; all emanate a brilliant light. This Bodhisattva Realm is an altruistic world, where those who are able to guide and save others reside.

Although those in the sixth dimension are remarkable and talented people, they still tend to concentrate on their own progress, aiming to develop themselves. However, the Bodhisattva Realm of the seventh dimension is a completely altruistic world where the inhabitants concentrate all their energy on thinking about how they can save others. I would like all people on earth to be able to return to this world. As your goal in life, I would like you to aim to return to this level. Otherwise, your success solely of this world will be of no significance. There are so many theories of success that deal only with worldly matters, but you must set your sights on being truly successful in both this world and the other. True success is to return to this glorious world of Bodhisattva.

The preparation required is the same as I described earlier. While on earth, begin your day with prayer, work to help lead others to true happiness, and learn the Truth eagerly. Encourage one another and live in harmony, while striving to fulfill the pledge to create the world of light, a Buddha Land, on earth, hand in hand with other people. Those who have lived like this will return to the world of Bodhisattva, and those who can rejoice in this work already have the Bodhisattva spirit.

Suppose the average age of readers of this book is about forty; in this case, you still have another forty years left to live. What is important is for you to be able to teach and guide as many people as possible, devoting yourself to be of service to many during these next forty years. If you can, aim to guide approximately ten thousand people. Try to invite them to the Truth, light a fire in their hearts, and save as many people as possible. If you are able to guide as many as ten thousand, you will be able to return to the Bodhisattva Realm. It is not easy, but quite possible to achieve through diligent effort.

Please make a plan for the remaining years of your

life, and guide about ten thousand people to the right path. Awaken them to the Truth, not letting them fall to hell, and encourage them to create a Utopia, an ideal world together. This is the surest way to develop your soul.

In another of my books, *Invincible Thinking*,[9] I have introduced a method for always winning in life, transforming any trouble or difficulty we encounter in this world into personal strength. In contrast, "the Philosophy of Progress" enables us to transcend this world, to develop our soul, society, and humankind from the perspective of the other world. This philosophy is not based on a worldly perspective; it is a way of thinking that makes you consider your work from the perspective of the world you will return to, elevating yourself and transforming this world into a world filled with light. This is the philosophy of progress.

Do not let yourself settle for a viewpoint belonging to this three-dimensional world. Change your perspective to that of the seventh-dimensional Bodhisattva Realm, and ask yourself deep in your heart what you should be doing, what work has to be done to create an ideal society on earth. Then the path to development will unfold of its own accord.

---

9. Refer to *Invincible Thinking* by Ryuho Okawa (Lantern Books, 2003).

# Postscript

Following *Invincible Thinking,* a bestseller in Japan, this book, *The Philosophy of Progress*, will similarly be welcomed by business people and others seeking success. Nothing is more exciting than the experience of development and progress. This book of lectures was published in Japan at a time when Happy Science was developing rapidly, becoming an organization of several million people.

This book tells the secrets of the miracle of rapid growth of Happy Science, experienced for the first time in the history of religion in Japan. The effectiveness of the message of this book has in a sense already been proven, and this message has the backing of my complete confidence in it. I hope that you also will have the experience of making true progress, both now and in the future.

Ryuho Okawa
President
Happy Science

# ABOUT THE AUTHOR

Ryuho Okawa, founder of Happy Science, Kofuku-no-Kagaku in Japan, has devoted his life to the exploration of the Truth and ways to happiness.

He was born in 1956 in Tokushima, Japan. He graduated from the University of Tokyo. In March 1981, he received his higher calling and awakened to the hidden part of his consciousness, El Cantare. After working at a major Tokyo-based trading house and studying international finance at the Graduate Center of the City University of New York, he established Happy Science in 1986.

Since then, he has been designing spiritual workshops for people from all walks of life, from teenagers to business executives. He is known for his wisdom, compassion and commitment to educating people to think and act in spiritual and religious ways.

He has published over 500 books, including *The Laws of the Sun, The Golden Laws, The Laws of Eternity, The Science of Happiness,* and *The Essence of Buddha.* His books have sold millions of copies worldwide. He has also produced successful feature-length films (including animations) based on his works.

The members of Happy Science follow the path he teaches, ministering to people who need help by sharing his teachings.

# LANTERN BOOKS BY RYUHO OKAWA

**The Laws of the Sun**: *Discover the Origin of Your Soul*
978-1-930051-62-1

**The Golden Laws**: *History through the Eyes of the Eternal Buddha*
978-1-930051-61-4

**The Laws of Eternity**: *Unfolding the Secrets of the Multidimensional Universe*
978-1-930051-63-8

**The Starting Point of Happiness**
*A Practical and Intuitive Guide to Discovering Love, Wisdom, and Faith*
978-1-930051-18-8

**Love, Nurture, and Forgive**: *A Handbook to Add a New Richness to Your Life*
978-1-930051-78-2

**An Unshakable Mind**: *How to Overcome Life's Difficulties*
978-1-930051-77-5

**The Origin of Love**: *On the Beauty of Compassion*
978-1-59056-052-5

**Invincible Thinking**: *There Is No Such Thing As Defeat*
978-1-59056-051-8

**Guideposts to Happiness**: *Prescriptions for a Wonderful Life*
978-1-59056-056-3

**The Philosophy of Progress**: *Higher Thinking for Developing Infinite Prosperity*
978-1-59056-057-0

**The Laws of Happiness**: *The Four Principles for a Successful Life*
978-1-59056-073-0

**Ten Principles of Universal Wisdom**
*The Truth of Happiness, Enlightenment, and the Creation of an Ideal World*
978-1-59056-094-5

**Tips to Find Happiness**
*Creating a Harmonious Home for Your Spouse, Your Children, and Yourself*
978-1-59056-080-8

*Order at www.lanternbooks.com*

# What is Happy Science?

Happy Science is an organization of people who aim to cultivate their souls and deepen their love and wisdom through learning and practicing the teachings (the Truth) of Ryuho Okawa. Happy Science spreads the light of Truth, with the aim of creating an ideal world on Earth.

Members learn the Truth through books, lectures, and seminars to acquire knowledge of a spiritual view of life and the world. They also practice meditation and self-reflection daily, based on the Truth they have learned. This is the way to develop a deeper understanding of life and build characters worthy of being leaders in society who can contribute to the development of the world.

# Events and Seminars

There are regular events and seminars held at your local temple. These include practicing meditation, watching video lectures, study group sessions, seminars and book events. All these offer a great opportunity to meet like-minded friends on the same path to happiness and for further soul development. By being an active participant at your local temples you will be able to:

- Know the purpose and meaning of life
- Know the true meaning of love and create better relationships
- Learn how to meditate to achieve serenity of mind
- Learn how to overcome life's challenges

*...and much more*

# International Seminars

International seminars are held in Japan each year where members have a chance to deepen their enlightenment and meet friends from all over the world who are studying Happy Science's teachings.

# Happy Science Monthly Publications

Happy Science has been publishing monthly magazines for English readers around the world since 1994. Each issue contains Master Okawa's latest lectures, words of wisdom, stories of remarkable life-changing experiences, up-to-date news from around the globe, in-depth explanations of the different aspects of Happy Science, movie and book reviews, and much more to guide readers to a happier life.

Hundreds of interesting back-issues of our Monthly publications are available at your nearest temple.

You can pick up the latest issue from your nearest temple or subscribe to have them delivered (*please contact your nearest temple from the contacts page*). Happy Science Monthly is available in many other languages too, including Portuguese, Spanish, French, German, Chinese, and Korean.

# Our Welcome e-Booklet

You can read our Happy Science Welcome Introductory Booklet and find out the basics of Happy Science, testimonies from members and even register with us:

http://content.yudu.com/Library/A1e44v/HappyScienceIntro

If you have any questions, please email us at:

**inquiry@happy-science.org**

# CONTACTS

**Find more information about locations, activities, and events offered at Happy Science by visiting the websites below**

## Japan
www.kofuku-no-kagaku.or.jp/en
**Tokyo**
1-6-7 Togoshi, Shinagawa,
Tokyo,
142-0041 Japan
Tel: 81-3-6384-5770
Fax: 81-3-6384-5776
tokyo@happy-science.org

## United States of America
**New York**
www.happyscience-ny.org
79 Franklin Street, New York,
New York 10013, U.S.A.
Tel: 1-212-343-7972
Fax: 1-212-343-7973
ny@happy-science.org

**Los Angeles**
www.happyscience-la.org
1590 E. Del Mar Blvd.,
Pasadena, CA 91106, U.S.A.
Tel: 1-626-395-7775
Fax: 1-626-395-7776
la@happy-science.org

**San Francisco**
www.happyscience-sf.org
525 Clinton St., Redwood City,
CA 94062, U.S.A
Tel: 1-650-363-2777
Fax: same
sf@happy-science.org

**New York East**
nyeast@happy-science.org

**New Jersey**
newjersey@happyscience.org

**Florida**
www.happyscience-fl.org
florida@happy-science.org

**Chicago**
chicago@happy-science.org

**Boston**
boston@happy-science.org

**Atlanta**
atlanta@happy-science.org

**Albuquerque**
abq@happy-science.org

**Hawaii**
www.happyscience-hi.org
hi@happy-science.org

**Kauai**
kauai-hi@happy-science.org

## Canada
**Toronto**
http://www.happy-science.ca
toronto@happy-science.org

**Vancouver**
vancouver@happy-science.org

## Europe
**London**
www.happyscience-eu.org
3 Margaret Street, London W1W
8RE, United Kingdom
Tel: 44-20-7323-9255
Fax: 44-20-7323-9344
eu@happy-science.org

## Oceania
**Sydney**
www.happyscience.org.au
sydney@happy-science.org

**Sydney East**
bondi@happy-science.org

**Melbourne**
melbourne@happy-science.org

**New Zealand**
newzealand@happy-science.org

To find out more Happy Science
locations worldwide, go to
http://www.kofuku-no-
kagaku.or.jp/en/page9.html

# Want to know more?

Thank you for choosing this book. If you would like to receive further information about titles by Ryuho Okawa, please send the following information either by fax, post or e-mail to your nearest Happy Science Branch.

1. Title Purchased

_____

2. Please let us know your impression of this book.

_____

_____

3. Are you interested in receiving a catalog of Ryuho Okawa's books?

       Yes ❑         No ❑

4. Are you interested in receiving Happy Science Monthly?

       Yes ❑         No ❑

Name : Mr / Mrs / Ms / Miss : _____

Address : _____

_____

_____

Phone: _____

Email: _____

_Thank you for your interest in Lantern Books._